# Gods Terrible Voice in the City!

# Gods Terrible Voice in the City!

By

Thomas Vincent

This book was written in the prevailing style of that period. Language and spelling have been left original in an effort to give the full flavor of this classic work.

Bottom of the Hill Publishing
Memphis, TN
www.BottomoftheHillPublishing.com

ISBN: 978-1-61203-629-8

# Content

Wherein you have:

I. The **Sound** of the Voice, in the *history* of the two late dreadful judgments of PLAGUE and FIRE in London.

II. The **Interpretation** of the Voice, in a discovery of the *cause* and *design* of these judgments.

*"Listen! The Lord's voice cries unto the city. The man of wisdom shall see Your name. Hear the rod, and the One who has appointed it!" —Micah 6:9*

To all such of the City, who have seen the desolations of London by the late judgments of *Plague* and *Fire.*

It might have seemed more seasonable unto some, if a work of this nature had come forth unto view more immediately after the sound of God's terrible voice of the last dreadful judgment of the fire; because if a man strikes while the iron is hot — it is likely to make the more deep impression; which, when it grows cool, grows hard and unmalleable. And if the *hammer of the Word* had been used, when London was newly come forth out of the fiery furnace — some might think they would have yielded the more easily unto its strokes, and the better have received the impression which this hammer would work them unto. And, since the fresh and lively remembrance of the judgment is more worn off; it is to be feared that they are more cooled and hardened, and therefore in likelihood it will be more difficult to effect a due impression of the judgments, by the Word, upon them.

Yet, besides that, it was not in my thoughts to attempt this work, until the greatest part of the winter was spent; I may further add, that though a discourse concerning the plague would have been most seasonable under the judgment itself, when people, who were generally taken off from their trading, had room and time for retirement and consideration, more than ever they had in their lives before; and therefore were more likely to lay to heart what might be spoken or written unto them on that subject; Yet the reason is not the same in the judgment of the fire, which (however startling and astonishing), was so far from giving them retiring time for consideration, as the former judgment of the plague had done; that it did engage them unto more laborious works than ever they had, not only while London was burning, in removing what they could save of their goods from the fire; but also since, in looking out for new habitations, and fitting their houses and shops for trades; which has given them occasion for so much distraction, that I fear they could hardly settle their minds to read and consider so seriously as they should, what the Lord has been doing with them, and speaking unto them by this Terrible Voice, which has sounded so loud in their ears.

But by this time I hope that the most have attained to some kind of settlement; at least, so much, as to give them time to sit down and ponder upon the meaning of God, in these strange and dreadful judgments of *plague* and *fire* in the city; and therefore this book may be more seasonable unto the most, than if it had been written and presented to them immediately after the fire had burnt them out of their habitations.

Friends, it is high time for all of you to retire yourselves, and bethink yourselves, and wisely to consider God's dealings with you; to open your ear, and labor to understand these *speaking judgments*, lest, if God be provoked by your deafness and incorrigibleness, to speak a third time — it be in your utter ruin and desolation! If these papers are any ways helpful to revive in your memories the judgments themselves, by the *Historical Narration* which here you have of them, to work your hearts to some sense of sin in discovery of the cause; and to persuade you to a ready compliance with God's design, in the declaring of what God now expects from you, after such dreadful executions; as yours will be the benefit — so I desire that God may have the whole glory; and that you would make this return for my help of you — to help me with your prayers, that I may be the more helpful to you in mine, who am, Your dearly affectionate friend, and servant in the Lord,

*Thomas Vincent*

*"By terrible things in righteousness, will you answer us!"*
—Psalm 65:5

# INTRODUCTION

"When a trumpet sounds in a city — do not the people tremble? *When disaster comes to a city — has not the Lord caused it?* The lion has roared — who will not fear? The Sovereign Lord has spoken — who can but prophesy?" —Amos 3:6, 8.

When the Pharisees spoke to our Savior to rebuke his disciples for their loud praises of the Lord with hosannas, He tells them, "If they should hold their peace, the stones would immediately cry out," Luke 19:39, 40. And we read in Habakkuk 2:11 "Of the stone crying out of the wall, and the beam out of the timber making answer."

Certainly we in London have lately heard the cry of stones and walls, of timber and beams in their fall and flames; I mean in the late dreadful fire, which has laid our Jerusalem in heaps! Or rather, we have heard the voice of God in this and other terrible things which have come upon us: let none then rebuke, if one so unfit, makes an attempt to speak something of the *meaning of London's fire*, or of God's terrible voice in this and other judgments, when by the mouth of babes God can declare his will.

# Section 1

## How God speaks

"By terrible things in righteousness, you will answer us."
—Psalm 65:5

This whole Psalm breathes forth nothing but grace and goodness unto the people of God, from the beginning of it, to the end; yes, in the verse of my text where God speaks most terribly and righteously it, the judgments and destructions which he brings upon their enemies — yet he is called the *God of their salvation*; and those *terrible things* by which God speaks, are not only a righteous answer unto their enemies' sins, but also a gracious answer unto his people's prayers: "By terrible things in righteousness, you will answer us."

I shall not speak of terrible things in the restrained sense, as they befall only the enemies of God's people, and the wicked, while the righteous do escape, and it may be hereby are preserved; but as they may befall *any* people, not excluding God's people, whom the Lord may answer by terrible things in righteousness.

Two doctrines we may observe:

Doctrine. 1. That God sometimes speaks unto a people by terrible things.

Doctrine. 2. That when God speaks most terribly — He answers most righteously

**First. That God sometimes speaks unto a people by terrible things.** Here I shall show,

1. *How* God may be said to speak.
2. *What* those terrible things are, by which God sometimes speaks.
3. *Why* God sometimes speaks unto a people by terrible things;
4. The *application.*

**1. How God may be said to speak.**

God, being a Spirit, has no *mouth* nor *tongue* properly as men have, who have bodies; and therefore his way of speaking is not like ours (though sometimes he has created a voice in as articulate a sound, as if it had proceeded from the mouth of man, to declare his will,) but there are several ways in which God has spoken, and speaks unto men, by which he does as really and effectually make known his mind, as if he spoke with man's voice.

1. God has spoken formerly unto men **immediately**, in extraordinary ways, and that sometimes more terribly; as when he gave the law upon Mount Sinai, when the Mount burned with fire, and there was blackness, and darkness, and tempest, thunderings and lightnings, and the sound of the trumpet exceeding loud, and the voice of words so exceeding terrible, that it made the whole camp to tremble; and Moses himself said, "I exceedingly fear and quake," Exodus 19:16; Hebrews 12:18-21.

This way of God's speaking, the children of Israel were not able to bear; therefore they desired that *Moses* might speak unto them; but that *God* would not speak unto them thus any more, lest they should die, Exodus 20:19.

At other times God spoke with a more still and gentle voice, and in a more mild way; as when he spoke to Samuel in the night, he thought at first that it had been the voice of Eli, 1 Samuel 3:4, 5. Thus God spoke unto Abraham, unto Jacob, unto Moses, to whom it is said, "He spoke face to face, as a man speaks to his friend," Exodus 33:11.

God spoke also in an extraordinary way to his prophets of old, when he made known unto them his counsel, that they might declare it unto the people;

- sometimes he spoke unto them with an audible voice, which he created when no shape was seen;
- sometimes by angels, who appeared in bodies, which they laid down again when they had delivered their message;
- sometimes by dreams and visions in the night;
- sometimes by Urim and Thummim;
- sometimes by more secret inspirations of the Spirit.

In the last days of God's extraordinary speaking, he spoke by the most extraordinary person, namely, by his own most dearly beloved, and only begotten Son, Hebrews 1:1, 2; whom he sent out of his bosom to declare himself, John 1:18; and reveal what he had heard of the Father, John 15:15, who brought life and immortality to light by the Gospel, and made known God's purpose and grace in man's salvation, 2 Tim. 1:9, 10; and uttered such things as were kept secret from the foundation of the world, Matthew 13:35.

The Gospel began to be spoken of by the Lord Jesus himself, and was continued and confirmed by his Apostles, who were his witnesses, to whom God also did bear witness with signs, and wonders, and divers miracles, and gifts of the Holy Spirit, according to his will, in such extraordinary ways.

Yet *still* God speaks unto men. There are two ways of God's speaking now unto men, namely, his *Word* and his *works*.

1. His Word contained in the Scriptures of the Old and New Testament, which holy men wrote as they were inspired by the Holy Spirit, 2 Peter 1:21. And thus God speaks either *externally* by his Word alone, or *internally* with his Word by his Spirit.

1. God speaks now unto men **externally** by his Word alone, to some more silently, unto whom he gives his Scriptures only to be read, and brings to their view his written Word alone, without the advantage of other ordinances, which might more powerfully declare unto them his will.

Unto others he speaks more *audibly*, where the Gospel sounds in their ears, and with the Scriptures God sends his ministers to preach unto them.

God speaks by his *ministers*, who are his *watchmen*, in his name to warn the people of his judgments temporal and eternal, which in the Scriptures he has threatened, Ezekiel 3:17, 18, etc.; Isaiah 62:6, who are the Lord's ambassadors, 2 Corinthians 5:20; from whom they have a commission to preach the Gospel, and declare the glad tidings of salvation unto all such as repent, and believe, and yield up themselves unto the obedience of the Word.

Ministers stand in the room of Christ; and it is well for us that God speaks unto us by ministers, because we would not be able to endure, should he speak unto us immediately by himself; should he speak unto us with an audible voice, as he did to the children of Israel on Mount Sinai, when he gave the law. This would be so terrible, that with them we would desire to hear Moses, and choose ministers, rather to speak unto us; yes, if Christ Jesus himself should come down from Heaven, however he might have been heard in his state of *humiliation*, when his *Deity* was so much veiled; yet if he should now appear in the *glory* he has with the Father, or as he appeared unto John his beloved disciple, when his eyes were as a flame of fire, and his countenance like the sun when it shined in its full strength, and his voice like the sound of many waters — I say, if Christ should thus appear, and preach unto us, such a *dread* and astonishment would fall upon us, that we should fall down dead at his feet, as his disciple John did, Rev. 1:13-17. Therefore it is better for us in this state of weakness, that God speaks to us by ministers, men of like passions and infirmities with ourselves, whom we may be able to bear up, and whose words, notwithstanding our weakness, we may be able to hear.

2. God now also speaks unto men **internally**, with his Word by his *Spirit*; when God sends his Spirit with his Word, for conviction only, or some common work. Thus God calls upon the wicked, who sit under the preaching of the Word, moves and strives with them by his Spirit, but they resist the Spirit, stifle convictions, and will not hearken to his calls and motions, Genesis 6:3; Acts 7:51.

But especially God speaks *with* his Word by his Spirit; when he sends his Spirit for *conversion*, and to effect a saving change: thus God speaks when he: calls blind sinners out of darkness into his marvelous light, 1 Peter 2:9; quickens dead sinners, putting into them a new principle of spiritual life, Ephesians 2:1; rescues enslaved sinners out of Satan's snare; 2 Tim. 2:26; delivering them from the power of the devil, and translating them into the kingdom of his dear Son, Colossians 1:13; when by his Spirit he draws sinners, John 6:44; and joins them unto Jesus Christ, 1 Corinthians 6:17.

God speaks unto men with his *Word* by his Spirit, when he does thus effectually call them; and he speaks unto men also by his Spirit, when he graciously visits those who are called, when he teaches, melts, warms, quickens, strengthened, and refreshes them by his Spirit, as they sit under the influence of his ordinances, when he speaks peace unto their consciences, shows them his reconciled face, shedding abroad his love in their hearts, and gives such sweet comforts, and ravishing joy as is unspeakable, and full of glory, John 6:45; John 14:26; Luke 24:32; Psalm 143:11; Ephesians 3:16; Acts 3:19; Psalm 85:8; Romans 5:5; Psalm 44:19; 1 Peter 1:8.

2. God speaks unto men by his **WORKS**; and that either by his works of creation, or by his works of providence.

1. God speaks by his works of CREATION. The *Heavens* have a voice, and declare God's glory, Psalm 19. 1; and the *earth* has not only an ear to ear, Isaiah 1:2; but also a tongue, as it were, to speak God's praise. We read of the *seas* roaring, and the *floods* clapping their hands; of the *mountains* singing, and the *trees* of the forest sounding forth their joyful acclamations; yes, animals, creeping things, and flying birds, creatures of the deeps; fire, hail, snow, rain, and stormy wind — as they fulfill his Word, so they speak, and in their way declare what their Maker is. Or rather in them, and by them God speaks, and make known something of himself, Psalm 148:7, 8, 10, etc.

We read of the voice of the Lord in *power*, the voice of the Lord in *Majesty*, the voice of the Lord upon the *waters*, the voice of the Lord dividing the *flames of fire*, the voice of the Lord shaking the wilderness of Kadesh, breaking the cedars of Lebanon, and the like — which is the voice of the Lord in the terrible noise of thunder, Psalm 29:8-8.

And there is no one work of the Lord (though not with such a noise) which does not with a loud voice, as it were, in the name of the Lord, proclaim unto the children of men how great and glorious the Lord is, who has given it its being, and use, and place in the world; especially the work of God in the *creation of Man*, his body, the members and senses; his soul (its powers and faculties) does without a tongue speak the praise of that God who curiously framed the body in the womb, and immediately infused the living soul, Psalm 139:14, 15; Zech. 12:1.

2. God speaks by his works of PROVIDENCE, and that both merciful and afflictive.

1. God speaks by his ***merciful*** providences; by his patience, and bounty, and goodness, He calls men unto repentance, Romans 2:4. He gives witness of himself, in giving rain and fruitful seasons, Acts 14:17.

God's *providing* mercies, God's *preventing* mercies, God's *preserving* mercies, God's *delivering* mercies; the number of God's mercies — which cannot be reckoned; the order and strange method of God's mercies — which cannot be declared; the greatness of God's mercies — in the kinds and strange circumstances which cannot be expressed — do all with open mouth call upon men from the Lord to repent of their sins which they have committed against him, and to yield all love, thankfulness, and obedience unto him.

2. God speaks by his ***afflictive*** providences: there is a *voice of God* in his *rod* — as well as in his Word, Micah 6:9, "Hear the rod, and He who has appointed it!" When God "chastens, he teaches," Psalm 44:12. When God lifts up his hand, and strikes — he opens his mouth also, and speaks; and sometimes opens men's ears too, and seals their instruction. Job 33:16.

Sometimes God speaks by rods more mildly, by lesser afflictions; sometimes God speaks by scorpions more terribly, by greater judgments: which leads to the second particular.

# Section 2

## What are those terrible things by which God sometimes speaks?

*Terrible things* are such great judgments of God, as do usually make a general impression of fear upon the hearts of people.

Take some instances.

1. The **PLAGUE** is a terrible judgment by which God speaks unto men. It is a *speaking judgment*; where God sends the plague — he speaks, and he speaks terribly; the plague is very terrible, as it effects terror. The *pestilence* which walks in darkness, is called the "terror by night," Psalm 91:5, 6.

The plague is very terrible, in that,

1. It is so *poisonous* a disease: it poisons the blood and spirits, breeds a strange kind of venom in the body, which breaks forth sometimes in boils, and ulcers, and great carbuncles; or else works more dangerously, when it preys upon the vitals more inwardly.

2. It is so *repulsive* a disease: it turns the good humours into putrefaction, which putting forth itself in the issues of running sores, gives a most repulsive smell. Such a disease for loathsomeness we read of, Psalm 38:5, 7, 11. "My wounds fester and are loathsome! My back is filled with searing pain; there is no health in my body. My loved ones and friends stay away, fearing my disease. Even my own family stands at a distance!"

3. It is so *infectious* a disease: it spreads itself worse than the *leprosy* among the Jews; it infects not only those which are weak, and infirm in body, and full of ill humours — but also those that are young, strong, healthful, and of the best health — and that sometimes sooner than others. The plague is infectious, and greatly infectious, whole cities have been depopulated through its spreading, many whole families have received infection, and death one from another thereby — which is the third thing that renders the plague so terrible.

4. It is so *deadly* a disease: it kills where it comes without mercy; it kills (I had almost said certainly;) very few do escape, especially upon its first entrance, and before its malignity is spent; few are touched by it — but they are killed by it. And it kills suddenly! It gives no warning before it comes; suddenly the arrow is shot

which, wounds unto the heart. So it gives little time of preparation before it brings to the grave. Under other diseases, men may linger out many weeks and months, or even years; but the plague usually kills within a few days; sometimes within a few hours after its first approach, though the body were ever so strong and free from disease before.

The plague is very terrible; it is terrible to those who have it; insomuch as it usually comes with *grim Death*, the king of terrors, in its hand! And it is terrible to those who do not have it, because of their *danger* of being infected by it; the *fear* of which has made such an impression upon some, that it has drained out of their hearts — all affections of love and pity to their nearest relations and dearest friends; so that when the disease has first seized upon them, and they have had the greatest need of support, they have left their friends in distress, and flown away from them, as if they had been their enemies!

2. A **DELUGE by water** is a *terrible judgment.* There have been several floods which we read of in histories, that have suddenly broken in upon some places, and overwhelmed habitations and inhabitants together.

But God never did, and never will speak so terribly by a deluge of water — as by the great deluge in the days of Noah, when the whole world was drowned thereby, excepting Noah, and those who were with him in the ark.

"In the sixth hundredth year of Noah's life, in the second month, and the seventeenth day of the month, in the same day were all the fountains of the great deep broken up." God withdrew the bounds which he had set to the great sea, so that the waters covered the earth as they did at the beginning, "and the windows of Heaven were opened," out of which God looked forth in anger upon the earth, and poured forth a "vial of his wrath," causing it to rain forty days and forty nights in dreadful showers, accompanied, as is probable, with stormy winds, and hideous tempests — which put the world into a fright and amazement! When the element of air seemed to be changed into water, and such a torrent flowed in upon them on every side, we may guess what *fear* they were overwhelmed with! But Noah and his family were safe in the ark, and the Lord "shut them in. For forty days the floodwaters grew deeper, covering the ground and lifting the boat high above the earth. As the waters rose higher and higher above the ground, the boat floated safely on the surface. Finally, the water covered even the highest mountains on the earth, rising more than twenty-two feet above the highest peaks. All the living things on earth died—birds, domestic animals, wild animals, small animals that scurry along the ground, and all the people. Everything that breathed and lived on dry land died. God wiped out every living thing on the earth—people, livestock, small animals that scurry along the ground, and the birds of the sky. All were destroyed. The only people who survived were Noah and those with him in the boat."

God spoke then terribly indeed unto the wicked world by the flood, which devoured them altogether in the midst of their security and sin; but God has promised he will never speak thus by water any more.

3. **FIRE** is another *terrible thing* whereby God sometimes is pleased to contend with a sinful people. Fire is very dreadful when it has a commission from God, and meets with much combustible matter, and prevails without resistance. God spoke terribly by fire unto *Sodom and Gomorrah*, when he rained fire and brimstone on those cities, and consumed them. "Then the Lord rained down fire and burning sulfur from the sky on Sodom and Gomorrah. He utterly destroyed them, along with the other cities and villages of the plain, wiping out all the people and every bit of vegetation. Abraham looked out across the plain toward Sodom and Gomorrah and watched as columns of smoke rose from the cities like smoke from a furnace!" Genesis 19.

God spoke terribly, though not so terribly, to Jerusalem, when he allowed their city to be set on fire by the Babylonians, and their temple to be burnt to the ground. See Jeremiah 52:12, 13.

But the most fearful instances of God's terrible voice by fire, are yet to come! Thus God will speak by fire unto *spiritual Babylon*, which may easily be proved to be Rome, from Rev. 17:18. She then being the great city, which reigned over the kings of the earth. Babylon's burning with fire you may read, "Therefore, these plagues will overtake her in a single day—death and mourning and famine. She will be *completely consumed by fire*, for the Lord God who judges her is mighty. And the kings of the world who committed adultery with her and enjoyed her great luxury will mourn for her as they see the smoke rising from her charred remains. They will stand at a distance, terrified by her great torment. They will cry out: How terrible, how terrible for you, O Babylon, you great city! In a single moment God's judgment came on you!" Revelation 18:8-10

God spoke terribly by fire when London was in flames, of which we will see in the application; but he will speak far more terribly when Babylon shall be in flames; and not only in part — but wholly, and utterly, and irreparably burnt, and turned into ashes: when not only the city shall be consumed — but also the Whore herself "shall be hated and made desolate, and devoured with fire by the kings of the earth," Rev. 17. 10.

The last instance of God's speaking terribly by fire will be the last day, when the Lord Jesus Christ, the judge of living and dead, shall come in glory, "This will happen when the Lord Jesus is revealed from Heaven in blazing fire with his powerful angels. He will punish those who do not know God and do not obey the gospel of our Lord Jesus. They will be punished with everlasting destruction and shut out from the presence of the Lord and from the majesty of his power!" 2 Thessalonians 1:7-9.

And the Apostle Peter tells us, that "the present Heavens and earth are reserved for fire, being kept for the day of judgment and destruction of ungodly men." 2 Peter 3:7.

Then God will speak terribly by fire, and above all, most terribly to the ungodly world; when he will sentence them unto, and cast them into the fire of Hell, where they must dwell with devouring fire, and inhabit everlasting burnings

4. The *sword of* ***WAR*** is a dreadful judgment, whereby God speaks sometimes very terribly; especially when he draws it forth against his own and his people's enemies. Hear how terribly God speaks in Deuteronomy 32:39-42. "See now that I myself am He! There is no god besides me. I put to death and I bring to life, I have wounded and I will heal, and no one can deliver out of my hand. I lift my hand to Heaven and declare: As surely as I live forever, when I sharpen my flashing sword and my hand grasps it in judgment, I will take vengeance on my adversaries and repay those who hate me!"

When God furbishes his sword, and sharpens it; when God girds his sword upon his thigh, and marches against his enemies; when he draws his sword, and makes slaughter with it; when his sword devours much flesh, and is made drunk with the blood of the slain; when God gives commission to the sword, saying, "Sword, go through such a land!" as Ezekiel 14:17. And "pours out his fury on the land in blood;" as verse 19. So that the *sword* is bathed in blood, and *garments* are rolled in blood, and the *land* is soaked in blood; when blood is poured forth like water, and dead bodies are cast forth into the open field without burial; and God makes an invitation to all feathered fowl to gather themselves together, and feast themselves upon the carcasses of the slain! as Ezekiel

29. 17-20. When God comes with "dyed garments from Bozrah," Is. 63:1. "When he gathers the nations, and brings them into the valley of Jehoshaphat, and there causes his mighty ones to come down against them." Joel 3:2-11. When the day of God's indignation comes, and he makes such a slaughter among his enemies, that the "earth stinks with their carcasses, and the mountains do melt with their blood," Isa, 34:2, 3. When God "treads the wine-press of his wrath, and the blood comes out of the wine-press, even to the horses' bridles," Rev. 14:20.

In a word, when the Lord shall come forth upon his white "horse" with his armies; and shall destroy the beast, and all the powers of the earth that take part with him; as Rev. 19. from the 11th verse to the end — then God will speak terribly indeed against his enemies by the sword, then he will "roar out of Zion, and utter his voice from Jerusalem," and that in such a manner, as will "make both the Heavens and the earth to tremble!" Joel 3:16

And indeed God speaks with a terrible voice, wherever he sends the *sword*, and makes the alarm of *war* to be heard; as sometimes he sends it among his own people for their sin, 1 Kings 8:38.

When God brings into a land a people of another language and religion, of a fierce countenance and cruel disposition; and gives them power to prevail, and brings the land under their feet, so that the mighty men are cut off by them, and the men of valor crushed in the gate; the young men fly and fall before them, and there is none to make any resistance; when they break in upon cities, plunder houses, ravish women and maids, strip and spoil, and put all to the sword, the young with the grey head, cruelly rip up women with child, and without any pity on little infants, dash them against the stones. God speaks more terribly by such a judgment, than by plague or fire!

5. The **FAMINE** is a dreadful judgment, whereby God speaks sometimes unto a people very terribly; when God "stretches upon a place the lines of confusion, and the stones of emptiness," as Isaiah 34:11. "I gave you empty stomachs in every city and lack of bread in every town! I also withheld rain from you when the harvest was still three months away. I sent rain on one town, but withheld it from another. One field had rain; another had none and dried up. People staggered from town to town for water but did not get enough to drink!" Amos 4:6-8

When God shoots into a land the *evil arrows of famine*, and it becomes exceeding sore; this is one of the most dreadful of all judgments in this world — far beyond plague, or fire, or sword.

See how pathetically the famine among the Jews is described, by Jeremiah in his Lamentations, "The parched tongues of their little ones stick to the roofs of their mouths in thirst. The children cry for bread, but no one has any to give them. The people who once ate the richest foods now beg in the streets for anything they can get. Those who once wore the finest clothes now search the garbage dumps for food. The guilt of my people is greater than that of Sodom, where utter disaster struck in a moment and no hand offered help. Our princes once glowed with health— brighter than snow, whiter than milk. Their faces were as ruddy as rubies, their appearance like fine jewels. But now their faces are blacker than soot. No one recognizes them in the streets. Their skin sticks to their bones; it is as dry and hard as wood. Those killed by the *sword* are better off than those who die of *hunger*. Starving, they waste away for lack of food from the fields. Tenderhearted women have cooked their own children. They have eaten them to survive the siege. But now the anger of the Lord is satisfied. His fierce anger has been poured out. He started a fire in Jerusalem that burned the city to its foundations!" Lamentations 4:4-12

6. The sixth terrible judgment is a **FAMINE OF THE WORD**, which is threatened, Amos 8:11, 12. "Behold, the days come, says the Lord, that I will send a famine in the land; not a famine of bread, nor a thirst for water — but of hearing the words of the Lord: and they shall wander from sea to sea, and from the north even to the east, and they shall run to and fro to seek the Word of the Lord, and shall not find it."

A famine of the Word is a worse judgment than a famine of bread! Indeed few do really think so, because the most judge according to sense; but that it is so, is evident to a man of faith and consideration: for as the soul is more excellent than the body, and the concernments of eternity, far beyond the concernments of this life: so the provisions for the soul are more excellent than the provisions for the body, and the means of getting eternal life, to be preferred before the means of preserving temporal life; and therefore by consequence the death and scarcity of provisions for the soul, must needs be a greater judgment than a scarcity of provisions for the body. Unto which I might add, that the famine of the Word usually brings with it many temporal judgments; the burning of the temple at Jerusalem, and the failing of vision was accompanied with slaughter by the sword, and captivity of the land.

7. And lastly, God speaks most terribly unto a people when he sends divers of these judgments together, as Lam. 1:20. "*Abroad*

the sword bereaves, at *home* there is death;" when enemies without, plague and famine within. God speaks terribly, when fire and sword go together; or sword and famine; or famine and plague; or famine of bread, and famine of the Word.

These are some of the terrible things by which God sometimes speaks.

# Section 3

## WHY is it, that the Lord speaks unto a people by such terrible things?

The reason is, because people do not hearken unto him, when speaking in any other way. "God speaks once, yes, twice — but men perceive it not," Job 33:14. God's *gentle* voice is not heard or minded — therefore he speaks more loudly and terribly, that people might be awakened to hear. Particularly God speaks thus terribly:

**1. Because people do not hearken to the voice of his Word and messengers.** God speaks audibly by ministers, and when they are not regarded, he speaks more feelingly by judgments! He speaks first by *threatenings*, and when they are slighted, he speaks by *executions*. God first lifts up his voice, and warns by his Word — before he lifts up his arm, and strikes with his rod! When men grow dull of hearing the sweet calls of the Gospel, God is even forced to thunder, that he may pierce their ear! When God speaks to the *ears* and they are shut — God speaks to the *eyes* and other *senses*, that his mind may be known. Especially when men obstinately refuse to hear — God is exceedingly provoked to execute his terrible judgments upon them. See Zech. 8:11, 12. "But they refused to pay attention; stubbornly they turned their backs and *stopped up their ears*. They made their hearts as hard as flint and would not listen to the law or to the words that the Lord Almighty had sent by his Spirit through the earlier prophets. So the Lord Almighty was very angry!"

So also when God gave up Jerusalem to desolation and ruin, see the sin which provoked the Lord hereunto, 2 Chron. 36:16. "They mocked the messengers of God, and despised his words, and misused his prophets, until the wrath of the Lord, arose against his people, until there was no remedy!"

**2. Because they do not hearken to the voice of his goodness and mercies.** The goodness and forbearance of God, speaks unto men from him, and call upon them to forbear sin for shame; to repent and return to him, Romans 1:4. But when men despise the riches of his goodness, and deafen their ear unto the language of his mercies, and trample his patience under foot, (though God has appointed a day of wrath *hereafter*, wherein he will reckon with the whole ungodly world together, and give them the just demerit of their sin,) yet sometimes his patience is turned hereby into fury, and his anger breaks forth into a flame, and consumes them by the blow of dreadful *temporal* judgments!

**3. Because they will not hearken to the voice of *lesser* afflictions.** When God's *Word* is not heard, he speaks by his *rod*. When his rod is not heard, he shoots with his arrows and strikes with his sword. And if *lesser afflictions* are not minded, then God speaks by more *dreadful awakening judgments*: as the sins of men do precede the judgments of God, so usually lesser judgments do precede greater judgments; and as there are degrees and steps which men usually do make before they arrive to a great height in sin — so there are degrees and steps which God usually takes, in inflicting his judgments for sin.

Look into one place for all, which shows how God proceeds from less to greater judgments, Lev. 26. from the 15th verse to the 40th. When his "statutes are despised, and covenant broken;" first he threatened to send upon them "consumption and a burning plague;" then he threatened that "they shall fall before their enemies;" and if "they will not hearken to his voice" in these judgments — he threatens to "punish them seven times more for their sins;" and to "make the Heavens as iron, and the earth as brass; and send a dearth among them." And if they will not "yet hearken," he threatens to "send wild beasts, which would devour their children and cattle." And if they would not be reformed by these things — but "still would walk contrary unto him," he threatens "to walk contrary unto them, and to punish them yet seven times more for their sins!" He threatens to bring a "sword upon them, to avenge the quarrel of his covenant; and when they should be gathered together in their cities, to "send the pestilence" among them: and hereunto to add the "famine." And if they would not yet "hearken unto God — but still walk contrary unto him," he threatens "that he will walk contrary to them in fury, and make them eat the flesh of their sons and their daughters, and lay waste their cities, and make their sanctuaries a desolation: and upon them that are left alive," he threatens "to send such faintness of heart, that they should flee at the sound of a shaken leaf, and fall when none pursued them; and that they should pine away in their iniquities in the land of their enemies.

Thus God proceeds by *steps* and *degrees*, in the execution of his fierce anger upon a rebellious people; when God speaks by ordinary diseases and is not heard — then sometimes he sends a plague! And if after a plague, people will not return to him who smites them, nor seek to pacify God's anger which is kindled against them, but walk so much the more contrary unto him — then he will walk contrary to them in fury, and send fire into their cities to devour their habitations! And if the voice of the fire is not heard, he has other judgments in readiness — sword, famine, and the like!

And if *temporal* judgments are not heeded — then he will bring upon them *eternal* judgments.

God is not heard any other way — therefore he speaks by such terrible things!

# Section 4

## The Application

God speaks sometimes to a people by terrible things.

These few last years have given sad instances hereof in England, especially the two last years in our city of London.

The voice of the Lord has been in the city, it has been loud and full of terror! the Lord has come forth against us with armed vengeance. Frowns have been in his brow; death and desolation in his looks; thunder has been in his voice; flames of fire in his hand! "The pestilence has gone before him, and burning coals at his feet!" Hab. 3:5. "The Lord thundered from Heaven; the voice of the Most High resounded. He shot his arrows and scattered the enemies, great bolts of lightning and routed them!" Psalm 18:13-14. "The Lord Almighty will come with thunder and earthquake and great noise, with windstorm and tempest and flames of a devouring fire!" Isaiah 29:6

Yes, "The Lord will make *his majestic voice* heard. He will display the strength of his mighty arm. It will descend with devouring flames, with cloudbursts, thunderstorms, and huge hailstones!" Isaiah 30:30. "Then the furrows of the earth were seen, and the foundations of the city were discovered, the earth also shook, because he was wroth, and the inhabitants trembled, because of his fierce anger; then the snares of death compassed us, and the fears of Hell got hold on us; and our hearts were moved within us, as trees when they are moved by the wind!"

Dreadful have God's late judgments been in London, the noise of which has gone forth, not only throughout the land — but also unto the outermost parts of the world.

Three things we should remark, in this terrible voice of God's judgments:

1. The *judgments* themselves.
2. The *cause* of the judgments.
3. The *design* of the judgments.

In the first, we have the **sound** of God's voice.

In the two last, the **interpretation** of God's voice.

**1. Concerning the judgments themselves.**

Here I might speak of the judgment executed, August 24, 1662, when so many ministers were put out of their places. I might speak of the judgments executed, March 24, 1665, when so many ministers were banished five miles from their churches; the former by way of introduction to the *plague* which some time after did spread in the land — but chiefly raged in the city; the latter by way of introduction to the *fire*, which quickly after did burn down London, the greatest city in England. These judgments having been so lately, and general in the land; and I presume, so generally known, with all their circumstances, it would be needless to give here a narration of them.

But this I must say, I could wish they were as generally believed to be *judgments*, and accordingly laid to heart: for I fear that the great insensibility, which people have been under of these judgments, because they have not reached the *flesh*, and their sottish inconsideration of God's dreadful displeasure herein, has provoked the Lord to send such judgments as have come nearer to sense — that they might perceive that God was angry indeed before, and that his greater displeasure in the former, might be known by his more sensible displeasure in the latter.

Let London seriously consider whether her Gospel-privileges were not her best defense against temporal calamities; and whether, since her slighting, abuse, and forfeiture, and God's seizure and stripping her so much of these — she has not been laid naked to those heavy strokes of extraordinary judgments which she has lately received.

London had the *Gospel ordinances* — powerful, pure, plentiful; ministers excellently qualified, and furnished with rare ministerial abilities. London had as many burning and shining lights, as any one such spot of ground under the scope of Heaven.

Not to speak of their abilities for preaching and defense of the truth: such gifts of prayer, London-ministers had, which were no small defense of the city, as I believe no city in the world could parallel.

O what prayers have there formerly been in London pulpits, especially on days of solemn humiliation! How have the spirits of ministers been carried forth sometimes in prayer for several hours together, (without vain repetitions) in such variety of affectionate enlargements, and with such raisedness and transports of spirit, as if they had been just leaving the body, and going to live and abide with God, and would converse no more with men or worldly things!

In their *confessions* of sin, how have they raked into the dunghill of a rotten heart, and laid abroad its inward filthiness! How have they traced the foot-steps of its deceitfulness, through the maze and wilderness of its many windings and turnings! How have they pierced into the very affections of sin, and ripped it up as it were, to the back-bone, bringing forth its very entrails to open view! How have they anatomized as it were the "body of death" in all the parts and members of it; discovering withal, the several diseases of every part, with their cause and manner of working! and all this in such pathetical cutting expressions, accompanied with such brokenness and bleeding of heart, as no mere *form* can imitate or effect.

In their supplications for the *pardon* of sin, for spiritual and Heavenly riches — O with what feeling and fervor did they express themselves! O with what faith and importunity did they wrestle and plead at the throne of grace for such favors, beyond the importunity of poor prisoners through the grates, or poor beggars at the doors, when they are most earnest for relief! Yes, how did they *besiege God* as it were, and seem "as if they would scale the walls of Heaven itself, and take the kingdom of Heaven with violence and force!" How have they even pressed in upon God with the dint of argument, and laid hold on him with the *hand of faith*, resolving not to let him go without a blessing!

In their supplications for the *church* and *land*, they have behaved themselves as if they had no private concernments. But how did they bear London upon their hearts when they came to the throne of grace! What yearning affections had they towards, and for the city! How many tears have they shed in bewailing her sins! How have they stood in the breach, when the Lord has been coming forth against this place! How have they held back his arm when it has been lifted up to strike! How have they stood "weeping between the porch and the altar, crying, spare your people, O Lord, and do not destroy London!" and many times have they prevailed to appease God's wrath, and turn away his fierce anger which has been kindled against us.

Gospel-ordinances, and Gospel-ministers were the safeguard of London, the glory and defense. But when the *ordinances* were slighted, and the *ministers* were mocked and misused by some who called themselves professors; and London did not yield the fruit which God looked for under such blessing (of which more when I come to speak of London's sins,) God is provoked not only to call some of his messengers home to himself — but also to allow the rest which were more conscientious, to be thrust into corners.

This did presage London's near approaching ruin and desolation, though few did believe it; and because they did not believe it, and were insensible of God's wrath in his judgment — therefore their danger was the greater of the other judgments which have come upon them. When so many *stakes* were plucked out — no wonder if the hedge is broken; when so many *pillars* were removed — no wonder if the building tumble to the ground.

But I proceed to give a ***narration*** *of the latter judgments of plague and fire.*

# Section 5

The **PLAGUE** so great, so recent, should not be forgotten; yet lest the Fire more recent, and proportionably more great, and the amazing fears, which since have risen within us, should shuffle former thoughts out of our minds, and raze out the impressions, which by the plague we had, and should labor to retain to our dying hour: therefore I shall give a *brief narration* of this sad judgment, and some observations of my own (who was here in the city from the beginning to the end of it) both to keep alive in myself and others, the memory of the judgment, that we may be the better prepared for compliance with God's design in sending the plague among us.

It was in 1665, that the Plague began in our city of London, after we were warned by the great Plague in Holland, in the year 1664, and the beginning of it in some remote parts of our land the same year; not to speak anything whether there was any signification and influence in the blazing stars not long before, that appeared in the view of London, and struck some amazement on the spirits of many. It was in the month of May that the Plague was first taken notice of; there were but of three who died of the disease in the whole year before; but in the beginning of May nine fell by the plague, one in the heart of the city, the other eight in the suburbs. This was the first arrow of warning that was shot from Heaven among us, and fear quickly begins to creep upon people's hearts; great thoughts and discourse there is in town about the plague, and they cast in their minds whether they shall go if the plague should increase. Yet when the next week, the decrease from nine to three, their minds are something appeased; discourse of that subject cools; fears are hushed, and hopes take place, that the black cloud did but *threaten*, and give a few drops; but the wind would drive it away. But when the number of the dead by the plague had amounted from three to fourteen, and then to forty-three, and the disease began so much to increase, and disperse.

Now *secure sinners* begin to be startled, and those who would have slept at quiet still in their nests, are unwillingly awakened. Now a great consternation seizes upon most people, and fearful forebodings of a desolating judgment. Now guilty sinners begin to look about them, and think with themselves into what corner of the land they might fly to hide themselves. Now the profane and sensual, if they have not remorse for their sins — yet dread and terrors, the effects of guilt, they could not drive from them; and if by company, and carousing, and carnal pleasures they do intoxicate and smooth their spirits in the day; yet we may guess what dread returns upon them, if they give but any room for retirement; and what hideous thoughts such people have in the silent night, through fears of death which they are in danger of.

Now, those who did not believe an unseen *God* — are afraid of unseen *arrows*; and those which slighted God's threatenings of eternal judgments — tremble at the beginning of his execution of one, and not the greatest temporal judgment. Now those who had as it were challenged the God of Heaven, and defied him by their horrid oaths and blasphemies, when he begins to appear — they retreat, yes fly away with terror and amazement. The *great orbs* begin first to move; the lords and gentry retire into their countries; their remote houses are prepared, goods removed, and London is quickly upon their backs: few ruffling gallants walk the streets; few spotted ladies to be seen at windows: a great forsaking there was of the adjacent places where the plague did first rage.

In June the number increased from 43 to 112; the next week to 168, the next to 267, the next to 470, most of which increase was in the remote parts; few in this month within or near the walls of the city; and few that had any note for goodness or profession, were visited at the first: God gave them warning to bethink and prepare themselves; yet some few who were choice were visited pretty soon, that the best might not promise themselves a reprisal, or interpret any place of Scripture so literally, as if the Lord had promised an absolute general immunity and defense of his own people from this disease of the plague.

Now, the citizens of London put to a stop in the career of their trade; they begin to fear whom they converse and deal with, lest they should have come out of infected places. Now roses and other sweet flowers wither in the gardens, are disregarded in the markets, and people dare not offer them to their noses lest with their sweet savor, that which is infectious should be attracted: and without some antidote, few stir abroad in the morning. Now many houses are shut up where the plague comes, and the inhabitants shut in, lest coming abroad they should spread infection. It was very dismal to behold the red crosses, and read in great letters, *Lord Have Mercy Upon Us*, on the doors; and such a solitude about those places, and people passing by them so gingerly, and with such fearful looks as if they had been lined with enemies in ambush, that waited to destroy them.

Now rich tradesmen prepare to depart; if they have not country houses, they seek lodgings abroad for themselves and families, and the poorer tradesmen, that they may imitate the rich in their fear, stretch themselves to take a country journey, though they have scarcely wherewithal to bring them back again. The ministers also (many of them) take occasion to go to their country-places for the summer time; or (it may be) to find out some few of their parishioners that were gone before them, leaving the greatest part of their flock without food or physic, in the time of their greatest need. (I don't speak of all ministers, those which did stay out of choice and duty, deserve true honor.) Possibly they might think *God* was now preaching to the city — and what was the need of *their* preaching? or rather did not the thunder of God's voice affrighten their guilty consciences and make them fly away, lest a bolt from Heaven should fall upon them, and spoil their preaching for the future; and therefore they would reserve themselves until the people had less need of them.

I do not blame any *citizens* retiring, when there was so little trading, and the presence of all might have helped forward the increase and spreading of the infection; but how did fear drive many away, where *duty* would have engaged them to stay in the place? Now the highways are thronged with passengers and goods, and London empties itself into the country; great are the stirs and hurries in London by the removal of so many families; fear puts many thousands on the wing, and those think themselves most safe, that can fly furthest off from the city.

In July the plague increases, and prevails exceedingly, the number of 470, which died in one week by the disease, arises to 715 the next week, to 1089 the next, to 1843 the next, to 2010 the next. Now the plague compasses the walls of the city like a flood, and pours in upon it. Now most parishes are infected both without and within; yet there are not so many houses shut up by the plague, as by the owners forsaking of them for fear of it; and though the inhabitants are so exceedingly decreased by the departure of so many thousands, the number of dying people increases fearfully. Now the countries keep guards, lest infectious people should from the city bring the disease unto them; most of the rich are now gone, and the middle sort will not stay behind: but the poor are forced (through poverty) to stay, and abide the storm. Now most faces gather paleness, and what dismal apprehensions do then fill their minds, what dreadful fears do then possess the spirits, especially of those whose consciences are full of guilt, and have not made their peace with God?

The old drunkards, and swearers, and unclean people are brought into great straits; they look on the right hand, and on the left, and death is marching towards them from every part, and they know not where to fly that they may escape it. Now death arrows begin to fly very thick about their ears! They see many fellow sinners fall before them. Every hour they themselves expect to be snatched away. And the very sinking fears they have had of the plague, has brought the plague and death upon many; some by the sight of a coffin in the streets, have fallen into a shivering, and immediately the disease has assaulted them, and *Sergeant Death* has arrested them, and locked the doors of their houses upon them, from whence they have come forth no more, until they have been brought forth to their graves!

We may imagine the hideous thoughts, and horrid perplexity of mind, the tremblings, confusions, and anguish of spirit, which some awakened sinners have had, when the plague has broke in upon their houses, and seized upon near relations, whose dying groans, sounding in their ears, have warned them to *prepare*; when their doors have been shut up and fastened on the outside with an inscription, "Lord have mercy upon us," and none are allowed to come in but a nurse, whom they have been more afraid of than the plague itself; when lovers, and friends, and companions in sin have stood aloof, and not dared to come near the door of the house, lest death should issue forth from thence upon them; especially when the disease has invaded themselves, and first began with a pain and dizziness in their head, then trembling in their other members; when they have felt boils to arise under their arms, and in their groins, and seen ulcers to come forth in other parts; when the disease has wrought in them to that height, as to send forth those spots which (most think) are the certain tokens of near approaching death; and now they have received the *sentence of death* within themselves, and have certainly concluded, that within a few hours they must go down into the dust, and their naked soul, without the case of their body, must make its passage into eternity, and appear before the highest Majesty, to render their accounts and receive their sentence!

None can utter the horror which has been upon the spirits of such, through the lashes and stings of their guilty consciences, when they have called to mind a life of sensuality and profaneness, their immorality, drunkenness, injustice, oaths, curses, derisions of saints and holiness, neglect of their own salvation; and when a thousand sins have been set in order before their eyes, with another aspect than when they looked upon them in the temptation; and they find God to be *irreconcilably angry* with them, and that the day of grace is over, the *door of mercy* is shut, and that pardon and salvation (which before they slighted) is now unattainable: that the *grave* is now opening its mouth to receive their bodies, and *Hell* opening its mouth to receive their souls; and they apprehend that they are now just entering into a place of endless woe and torment, and they must now take up their lodgings in the infernal regions of utter darkness, with devils, and their fellow-damned sinners, and there abide for evermore in the extremity of misery, without any hopes or possibility of a release; and that they have foolishly brought themselves into this condition, and been the cause of their own ruin; we may guess that the despairing agonies and anguish of such awakened sinners, has been of all things the most unsupportable; except the very future miseries themselves, which they have been afraid of.

In August how dreadful is the increase: from 2010, the number amounts up to 2817 in one week; and thence to 3880 the next; thence to 4237 the next; thence to 6102 the next!

Now the cloud is very black, and the storm comes down upon us very sharp. Now *Death* rides triumphantly on his *pale horse* through our streets; and breaks into almost every house, where any inhabitants are to be found. Now people fall as thick as leaves from the trees in autumn, when they are shaken by a mighty wind. Now there is a dismal solitude in London's streets. Now shops are shut in; very few people walk about, insomuch that the grass begins to spring up in some places, and a deep silence almost in every place, especially within the walls; no rattling coaches, no prancing horses, no calling in customers, nor offering wares; no *London Cries* sounding in the ears: if any voice is heard, it is the *groans* of dying people, breathing forth their last: and the *funeral knells* of those who are ready to be carried to their graves. Now most of the *well* are mingled among the *sick*, who otherwise would have got no help. Now in some places where the people did generally stay, not one house in a hundred that is not infected; and in many houses half the family is swept away; in some the whole, from the eldest to the youngest are swept away; few escape with the death of but one or two! Never did so many husbands and wives die together; never did so many parents carry their children with them to the grave, and go together into the same house under earth, who had lived together in the same house upon it. Now the nights are too short to bury the dead; the long summer days are spent from morning unto the twilight in conveying the vast number of dead bodies unto the bed of their graves.

Now we could hardly go forth — but we would meet many coffins, and see diseased people with sores and limping in the streets; among other sad spectacles, methought two were very affecting: one of a woman coming alone, and weeping, by the door where I lived (which was in the midst of infection) with a little coffin under her arm, carrying it to the new church-yard: I did judge that it was the mother of the child, and that all the family besides was dead, and she was forced to bury with her own hands, this her last dead child. Another, was of a man at the corner of the Artillery wall, that, as I judge, through the dizziness of his head with the disease, which seized upon him there, had dashed his face against the wall, and when I came by, he lay hanging with his bloody face over the rails, and bleeding upon the ground; and as I came back, he was removed under a tree in Moorfields, and lay upon his back; I went and spoke to him; he could make me no answer — but rattled in the throat, and, as I was informed, within half an hour died in the place.

It would be endless to speak what we have seen and heard of some in their frenzy, rising out of their beds, and leaping about their rooms; others crying and roaring at their windows; some coming forth almost naked, and running into the streets! Strange things have others spoken and done, when the disease was upon them; but it was very sad to hear of one who being sick alone, and was frantic, burnt himself in his bed.

Now the plague had broken in much among my own acquaintances; and of about sixteen or more whose faces I used to see every day in our house, within a little while I could find but four or five of them alive; scarcely a day passed over my head, for I think a month or more together — but I would hear of the death of someone or more whom I knew. The first day — that they were smitten; the next day — some hopes of recovery; and the third day — that they were dead.

In September, when we hoped for a decrease, because of the season, because of the number gone, and the number already dead; yet it was not come to its height — but from 6102, who died by the plague the last week of August, the number is augmented to 6988 in the first week in September; and when we conceived some little hopes in the next week's abatement, our hopes were quite dashed again, when the next week it did rise to 7165, which was the highest toll, and a dreadful toll it was! and of the 130 parishes in and about the city, there were but four parishes which were not infected; and in those, few people remaining that were not gone into the country.

Now the grave opens its mouth without measure; multitudes! multitudes! in the valley of the shadow of death thronging daily into eternity; the church-yards now are so stuffed with dead corpses, that they are in many places swelled two or three feet higher than they were before; and new ground is broken up to bury the dead.

Now "Hell from beneath is moved" at the number of the guests that are received into its chambers; the number of the wicked which have died by the plague, no doubt, has been far the greatest, as we may reasonably conclude, without breach of charity. And it is certain, that all the wicked who then died in sin were turned into Hell; how then are the damned spirits now increased! Some were damning themselves a little before in their oaths — and God is now damning their souls for it, and is passing the irreversible sentence of damnation upon them. Some were drinking wine in bowls a little before, and strong drink without measure; and now God has put another cup into their hands, a cup of red wine, even the wine of the wrath and fierceness of the Almighty! Some were a little before feasting their senses, pleasing their appetite, satisfying the desires of the flesh, and being past feeling, had given themselves up to lasciviousness, to work all immorality with greediness; but now their laughter is turned into mourning, and their joy into howling and woe; and they have recovered their *feeling* again — but instead of the *pleasures* which they felt, and their sensual delights, which took away the feeling of their consciences — they are made to feel the heavy hand of God; and to endure such anguish and horror, through the sense of God's wrath, as no tongue can express!

Now the *atheists* believe there is a God, and the anti-scripturists are convinced of the truth of God's Word — by the execution of God's threatenings in the Word upon them. Now the covetous and unjust, the malicious and cruel, the scoffers and profane — begin to suffer the vengeance of eternal fire: and the ignorant person with the merely religious, are not excused; yes, the hypocrites, with all impenitent and unbelieving people, are sent down to the place of weeping: and surely Hell wonders to see so many come among them from such a city as London, where they have enjoyed such *plenty* of such powerful means of grace; and place is given to them, even the *lowest* and *hottest*, where *Judas* and others are of the chief note.

Yet Hell does not engross all that die by the visitation; some there are (though not the first or most) who have room made for them in the mansions which are above.

The plague makes little difference between the *righteous* and the *wicked*, (except the Lord by a peculiar providence shelters some under his wing, and compasses them with his favor, as with a shield, hereby keeping off the darts that are shot so thick about them,) yet as there is little difference in the *bodies* of the righteous, and of others; so this disease makes little discrimination, and not a few fearing God are cut off among the rest; they die of the same distemper with the most profane, they are buried in the same grave, and there sleep together until the morning of the resurrection.

But as there is a difference in their spirits while they live, so there is a difference, and the chief difference, in their place and state after their separation from the body. Dives is carried to Hell — and Lazarus to Abraham's bosom, though he died with his body full of sores! Devils drag away the souls of the wicked after they have received their final doom at the bar of God — into utter darkness, where there is weeping, and wailing, and gnashing of teeth!

But angels convey the souls of the *righteous* into the Heavenly paradise, the New Jerusalem which is above, where God is in his glory; and the Lord Jesus Christ at his right hand, and a thousand thousands stand before him, and ten thousand, times ten thousand administer unto him, even an innumerable company of angels; and where the spirits of all just men and women made perfect, were before gathered; where there is fullness of joy, and rivers of eternal pleasures running about the throne of God, the streams of which do make glad all the inhabitants of New Jerusalem.

Now the weak prison doors of the body are broken down, and the strong everlasting gates of their Father's palace are lifted up, and the saints are received with joy and triumph, into glory; and they come with singing into Zion, and everlasting joy in their hearts, and all sorrow and sighing flees away like a cloud, which never any more shall be seen. Now the veil is rent, and they enter the Holy of Holies, where God dwells, not in the darkness of a thick cloud, as in the temple of old — but in the brightness of such marvelous light and glory, as their eyes never did behold, neither could enter into their heart to conceive; there they have the vision of God's face without any eclipse!

There they have the treasures of God's love opened, and his arms to receive them with dearest and sweetest embracements; which kindles in their hearts such a flame of love, so ravishing and delightful, as words cannot utter!

There they are entertained by the Lord Jesus Christ, whom in the world they have served; and he who showed them his grace, whom they had wondered at when they were in the body — does now show them his glory, which they wonder at much more. There they are welcomed by angels, who rejoice, if at their conversion, much more at their *coronation!* There they sit down with Abraham, Isaac, and Jacob, in the kingdom of their Father! There they find Moses, and David, and Samuel, and Paul, and all the holy martyrs and saints, which have died before them, among whom they are numbered and placed, who rejoice in their increased society.

And as there is a great difference between the condition of the souls of the righteous and the wicked, who died by the same disease of the plague, after their death and separation; so there is a great difference between the posture of their spirits at their death, and upon their sick-bed. Some wicked men are stupid and senseless, and are given up to a judicial hardness, and die in a sleep of carnal security, out of which they are not awakened, until they are awakened in the midst of flames! Others more sensible, and considering what is coming upon them, are filled with inexpressible terror, through the roarings and tearings of a guilty accusing conscience, and the fore-thoughts of that horrible unsupportable torment they are so near unto! Now scaring dreams do terrify them, and fearfulness of the bottomless pit, and the burning lake below, does surprise them; and some break forth in the anguish of their despairing souls, "Who can dwell with devouring fire, who can inhabit everlasting burnings?" And however jovial and full of pleasure their life has been — yet at their latter end — they are utterly consumed with terrors.

But mark the perfect man, and behold the *upright* — the end of that man is peace; whatever storms they have had in their passage through a rough sea, the wind blowing, and the waves roaring, and sometimes have been ready to sink through opposition and discouragement, sometimes have been overwhelmed with grief and doubtings, sometimes have been dashed upon the rocks of terror and perplexity; yet now they are come to the haven of death, the winds are hushed and still, the waves are smooth and silent, the storm is over, and there is a great calm upon their spirits; they are past the rocks, and are out of the danger they feared, when they are in the greatest danger of approaching death.

It was generally observed among us, that God's people who died by the plague among the rest, died with such peace and comfort, as Christians do not ordinarily arrive unto, except when they are called forth to suffer martyrdom for the testimony of Jesus Christ. Some who have been full of doubts and fears, and complaints while they have lived and been well, have been filled with assurance, and comfort, and praise, and joyful expectation of glory — when they have lain on their death-beds by this disease. And not only more mature Christians, who have been more ripe for glory, have had these comforts — but also some younger Christians, whose acquaintance with the Lord has been of no long standing.

I can speak something of my own knowledge concerning some of my friends whom I have been with. I shall instance only in the house where I lived. We were eight in family, three men, three youths, an old woman, and a young maiden — all which came to me, hearing of my stay in town, some to accompany me, others to help me. It was the latter end of September before any of us were touched; the young ones were not idle — but improved their time in praying and hearing, and were ready to receive instruction, and were strangely borne up against the fears of the disease and death, every day so familiar to the view. But at last we were visited, and the plague came in dreadfully upon us; the cup was put into our hand to drink, after a neighbor family had tasted it, with whom we had much sweet society in this time of sorrow. And first our young maiden was smitten, it began with a shivering and trembling in her flesh, and quickly seized on her spirits; it was a sad day, which I believe I shall never forget; I had been abroad to see a friend in the city, whose husband was newly dead of the plague, and she herself visited with it; I came back to see another whose wife was dead of the plague, and he himself under apprehensions that he should die within a few hours: I came home, and the maiden was on her death-bed, and another crying out for help, being left alone in a sweating fainting fit. What was a saving interest in Christ worth then? What a privilege to have a title to the kingdom of Heaven?

But I proceed. It was on the Monday when the maiden was smitten; on Thursday she died full of Heavenly tokens: on Friday one of the youths had a swelling in his groin; and on the Lord's day died with the marks of the distemper upon him: on the same day another youth did sicken, and on the Wednesday following he died: on the Thursday night his master fell sick of the disease, and within a day or two was full of spots — but strangely beyond his own, and others expectations, recovered. Thus did the plague follow us, and came upon us one by one: as Job's messengers came one upon the heels of another, so the *messengers of death* came so close one after another, in such dreadful manner, as if we must all follow one another immediately into the pit.

Yet the Lord in mercy put a stop to it, and the rest were preserved. But that which was very remarkable in this visitation, was the behavior especially of those youths that died, who I believe were less troubled themselves, than others were troubled for them. The first youth that was visited, being asked by his father concerning the provision he had made for his death and eternity; told him, he hoped, if he died, he would go to Heaven; being asked the grounds of his hopes, said, the Lord had enabled him to look beyond the world; and when he was drawing near to his end, boldly inquired whether the tokens did yet appear, saying, that he was ready for them, and so a hopeful bud was nipped. But let not the father or the mother weep, and be in sadness for him, he is, I do not doubt, with his Heavenly Father, which may be their comfort.

The other also was a very sweet hopeful youth, so loving and kind, that he could not choose but attract love from those that were acquainted with him; but the grace he had gotten in those years, being I suppose under seventeen, did above all beautify him, and stand him in the greatest stead; in his sickness he had much quiet and serenity upon his spirit, and lay so unconcerned at the thoughts of approaching death, that I confess I marveled to see it; the sting and fear of death were strangely taken out, through the hopes which he had of future glory; yet once he told his mother he could desire to live a little longer, if it were the will of God. She asked him why he desired it? He told her he desired to live until *fire* and *faggot* came; and above all, he would gladly die a martyr. She said, if he died now, he would have a crown: he answered — but if he died a martyr, he would have a more glorious crown; yet he was not unwilling to receive his crown presently; and went away with great peace and sweetness in his looks, to his Father's house; and I could not blame the mother's grief for the loss of such an only son; but to be so immoderate, was not well: now I am sure it is time to dry up tears, and lay aside sorrows for the loss of him who has been so long filled with joys in the Heavenly mansions.

I might speak of the bearing of the master in his sickness, under the apprehensions of death, when the spots did appear on his body, he sent for me, and desired me to pray with him; told me he was now going home, desired me to write to his friends, and let them know, that he did not regret his stay in the city, though they had been so importunate with him to come away; but he had found so much of God's presence in his abode here, that he had no reason to regret. He told me where he would like to be buried, and desired me to preach his funeral sermon on Psalm 16, "In your presence is fullness of joy, and at your right hand there are pleasures for evermore."

But the Lord raised him again beyond the expectation of himself, friends, or physician. Let him not forget God's mercies, and allow too much worldly business to crowd in upon him, and choke the remembrance and sense of God's goodness so singular; but let him show by his singularity in meekness, humility, self-denial and love, zeal, and holy walking — that the Lord has been singularly gracious unto him.

The plague now increased exceedingly, and fears there were among us, that within a while there will not be enough alive to bury the dead, and that the city of London will now be quite depopulated by this plague.

Now some ministers (formerly put out of their places, who did abide in the city, when most of ministers in places were fled and gone from the people, as well as from the disease, into the country) seeing the people crowd so fast into the grave and eternity, who seemed to cry as they went, for spiritual physicians; and perceiving the *churches* to be open, and *pulpits* to be open, and finding pamphlets flung about the streets — they judged that the law of God and nature did now command their preaching in public places, though the law of man did forbid them to do it. Surely if there had been a law that none should practice medicine in the city — but such as were licensed by the College of Physicians; I and most of those, when there was the greatest need of them, should in the time of the plague have retired into the country, and other physicians who had as good skill in medicine, and no license, would have stayed among the sick — none would have judged it to have been breach of law, in such an extraordinary case, to endeavor by their practice, though without a license, to save the lives of those who by good care and medicine, were capable of a cure. And they could hardly have freed themselves from the guilt of murder of many bodies, if for a nicety of law, in such a case of necessity, they would have neglected to administer the remedy. The case was the same with the unlicensed ministers who stayed, when so many of the licensed ones were gone, and as the need of *souls* was greater than the need of bodies, the sickness of the one being more universal and dangerous than the sickness of the other; and the saving or losing of the soul, being so many degrees beyond the preservation or death of the body; so the obligation upon ministers was stronger, and the motive to preach, greater; and for them to have incurred the guilt of *soul-murder*, by their neglect to administer soul-remedies, would have been more heinous and unanswerable: that they were called by the Lord into public, I suppose that few of any seriousness will deny, when the Lord did so eminently own them, in giving many seals of their ministry unto them.

Now they are preaching, and every sermon was unto them, as if they were preaching their last. *Old Time* seems now to stand at the head of the pulpit, with its great scythe; saying with a hoarse voice, *"work while it is called today, at night I will mow you down!"* *Grim Death* seems to stand at the side of the pulpit, with its sharp arrow, saying, *"shoot God's arrows, and I will shoot mine!"* The *grave* seems to lie open at the foot of the pulpit, with dust in her bosom, saying,

Louden your cry
To God, To men,
And now fulfill your trust:
Here you must lie,
Mouth stopped,
Breath gone,
And silent in the dust!

Ministers now had awakening calls to seriousness and fervor in their ministerial work; to preach on the *side and brink of the pit of Hell* — into which thousands were tumbling; to pray under such near views of eternity, into which many passengers were daily entering, might be a means to stir up the spirit more than ordinary.

Now there is such a vast concourse of people in the churches where these ministers are to be found, that they cannot many times come near the pulpit doors for the press — but are forced to climb over the pews to them: and such a face is now seen in the assemblies, as seldom was seen before in London; such eager looks, such open ears, such greedy attention — as if every word would be eaten which dropped from the mouths of the ministers.

If you ever saw a *drowning man catch at a rope*, you may guess how eagerly many people did catch at the Word, when they were ready to be overwhelmed by this overflowing scourge which was passing through the city! When death was knocking at so many doors; and God was crying aloud by his judgments; and ministers were now sent to knock, cry aloud, and lift up their voice like a trumpet — then, then the people began to open the ear and the heart, which were fast shut and barred before. How did they then hearken as for their lives, as if every *sermon* were their last, as if *death* stood at the door of the church, and would seize upon them so soon as they came forth; as if the *death arrows* which flew so thick in the city would strike them before they could get to their houses; as if they were immediately to appear before the judgment bar of that God — who by his ministers was now speaking unto them!

Great were the *impressions* which the Word then made upon many hearts, beyond the power of man to effect, and beyond what the people before ever felt, as some of them have declared: "When sin is ripped up and reproved!" O the *tears* that slide down from the eyes, when the judgments of God are denounced. O the *tremblings* which are upon the conscience, when the Lord Jesus Christ is made known and offered! O the longing desires and openings of heart unto him, when the riches of the *Gospel* are displayed, and the *promises* of the covenant of grace are set forth and applied! O the inward burnings and sweet flames which were in the affections!

Now the *net* is cast, and many *fish* are taken! Now the *pool* is moved by the angel, and many leprous spirits, and sin-sick souls, are cured! Now many were brought to the birth, and born again. A strange moving there was upon the hearts of multitudes in the city; and I am persuaded that many were brought over effectually unto saving faith in Jesus Christ; whereof some died by the plague with willingness and peace; others remain steadfast in God's ways unto this day.

But *convictions* many hundreds had, if not thousands, "with the dog returned to their vomit," and with the sow, "have wallowed again in the mire" of their former sins.

The work was the more great, because the *instruments* made use of were more obscure and unlikely; whom the Lord did make choice of the rather, that the glory by ministers and people might be ascribed in full unto himself.

About the beginning of these ministers preaching, especially after their first Fast together, the Lord began to remit and turn his hand, and cause some abatement of the disease.

From 7155 which died of the plague in one week, there is a decrease to 5538 the next, which was at the latter end of September; the next week a farther decrease to 4929, the next to 4327, the next to 2665, the next to 1421, the next to 1031; then there was an increase the first week in November to 1414 — but it fell the week after to 1050, and the week after to 652, and the week after that to 333; and so lessened more and more to the end of the year.

Then we had a toll of 97,306 who died, which was an increase of more than 79,000, over what it was the year before; and the number of those who died by the plague was reckoned to be 68,596 this year; when there were but 6 which the toll speaks of, who died the year before.

Now the citizens, who had dispersed themselves abroad into the countries, because of the contagion, think of their old houses and trades, and begin to return, though with fearfulness and trembling, lest some of the *after-drops of the storms* should fall upon them. And O that many of them had not brought back their old *hearts* and *sins*, which they carried away with them! O that there had been a general *repentance* and reformation, and returning to the *Lord* who had smitten the city! The Lord gave them leisure and vacation from their trades for the *one necessary* thing; which had they improved, and generally mourned for sin, which brought the plague upon the city, had they humbly and earnestly sought the Lord to turn from his fierce anger, which was kindled against London — it might have prevented the desolating judgment by fire!

But alas! how many spent their time of leisure in toys and trifles, at best about feeding and preserving their bodies — but no time in serious minding the salvation of their souls; and if some were a little awakened with fear, while the plague raged so greatly, and they looked upon themselves to be in such danger; yet when they apprehended the danger to be over — they dropped *asleep* faster than before! Still they are the same or worse than formerly: those who were drunken — are drunken still; those who were filthy — are filthy still; and those who were unjust and covetous — do still persevere in their sinful course: cozening, and lying, and swearing, and cursing, and pride, and envy, and flesh-pleasing, and the like God-displeasing, and God-provoking sins (of which in the catalogue of London sins) do abound in London, as if there were no signification in God's judgments by the plague!

Some return to their houses, and follow their *worldly business*, and work as hard as they can to make up the time that they have lost, without minding and laboring to improve by the judgment, and God's wonderful preservation of them. Others return, and *sin* as hard as they can, having been taken off for a while, from those opportunities and free liberties for sin, which they had before. But most began now to sit down at rest in their houses when the summer was come, and the plague did not return, and they bring back all their goods they had carried into the country because of the plague; they did not imagine they should be forced to remove them again so soon.

Thus concerning the *great Plague* in London.

# Section 6

"At the time of your appearing you will make them like a fiery furnace. In his wrath the Lord will swallow them up, and his fire will consume them." Psalm 21:9

I proceed next to give a narration of the judgment of the **FIRE**; in which I shall be more brief, it being dispatched in fewer days, than the plague was in months.

It was the 2nd of September 1666, that the anger of the Lord was kindled against London, and the fire began! It began in a baker's house in Pudding Lane — and now the Lord is making London "like a fiery furnace!" In his wrath, he devours and swallows up our habitations. It was in the depth and dead of the night, when most doors and senses were locked up in the city, that the fire broke forth and appeared abroad; and like a mighty giant refreshed with wine, awakes and arms itself, quickly gathers strength, when it had made havoc of some houses, rushes down the hill towards the bridge, crosses Thames Street, invades Magnus Church at Bridge-Foot, and though that church were so great — yet it was not a sufficient barricade against this invincible conqueror; but having scaled and taken this fort, it shoots flames with so much the greater advantage into all places round about; and a great building of houses upon the bridge is quickly thrown to the ground; then the *conqueror* being stayed in his course at the bridge, marches back towards the city again, and runs along with great noise and violence through Thames Street, westward, where, having such combustible matter in its teeth, and such a fierce wind upon its back — it prevails with little resistance, unto the astonishment of the beholders!

My business is not to speak of the *hand of man*, which was made use of in the beginning and carrying on of this fire. The beginning of the fire at such a time, when there had been so much hot weather, which badly dried the houses, and made them the more *fit for fuel*; the beginning of it in such a place, where there were so many *timber-houses*, and the shops filled with so much combustible matter; and the beginning of it just when the *wind* did blow so fiercely upon that corner towards the rest of the city, which then was like tinder to the sparks — this smells of a *popish design*, hatched in the same place where the *Gunpowder-plot* was contrived, only that this was more successful.

The world sufficiently knows how analogous this is to *popish principles and practices*; those, who could intentionally blow up king and parliament by gunpowder, might (without any scruple of their kinds of conscience) actually burn a heretical city (as they consider it) into ashes! For besides the orders they can have from *his Holiness*, (or rather *his Wickedness*) the pope, for the most horrid crimes of murder, incest, and the like; it is not unlikely — but they count such an action as this *meritorious*, (in *their* kind of merit) which, in the outcome, they will find to *merit* the flames of eternal fire, instead of a crown of glory, which I wonder that in their way they can have the least hopes of!

I believe that the people will now take more heed of them and their ways; and instead of promoting their cause — I hope that a contrary effect is produced; and that the before indifference of a generation more newly sprung up, who did not know them — is now turned into *loathing* and *detestation* of such a religion — as can allow of such heinous practices. My work is not to declare what has been proved against the papists, before the honorable committee of parliament appointed to inquire into their insolencies; and the proofs which have been given in, concerning the fire, and who have been accessory thereunto.

No! I would rather endeavor to turn people's eyes from *men* — to *God*; for whoever were the *instruments* — God was the *author* of this evil which has come upon us; there being no evil in the city (that is, evil of *punishment*) which the Lord as a righteous, and the supreme Judge, does not inflict.

And surely more of the extraordinary hand of God, than of any men, did appear in the burning of the City of London. God could have prevented men, by *unveiling* their plots (as he did that of the gun-powder treason) before they had taken effect. God could have directed and given a blessing unto means for the *quenching* of it when it was first kindled. God, who has the *winds* in his fist, could have gathered in the wind, and laid it asleep; or so turned it the other way, that it would have been a defense to the city. Or God, who has the *clouds* at his command, and the *bottles of Heaven* in his hand — could have gathered his thick clouds together, and squeezed them; he could have opened his *bottles*, and poured down *rain* in abundance upon the city; so that if the wind had blown as it did — it would have blown *water* upon the fire, which would quickly have put it out! But the Heavens at that time were brass — no showering clouds to be seen!

The fire begins, is quickly taken notice of, though in the midst of the night. *"Fire! fire! fire!"* resounds in the streets! Many citizens startle out of their sleep, look out of their windows, some dress themselves, and run to the place. The Lord Mayor of the city comes with his officers, a confusion there is, counsel is taken away; and London, so famous for wisdom and dexterity, can now find neither *brains* nor *hands* to prevent its ruin. The *hand of God* was in it! The decree was come forth: *"London must now fall — and who could prevent it?"*

No wonder when so many *pillars* are removed, if the building tumbles! The prayers, tears, and faith, which sometimes London has had — might have quenched the violence of the fire; might have opened Heaven for *rain*, and driven back the *wind*. But now, the fire gets mastery, and burns dreadfully! And God with his *great bellows* blows upon it, which makes it spread quickly, and go on with such force and rage, overturning all so furiously — that the whole city is brought into jeopardy of desolation!

That night, most of the Londoners had taken their last *sleep* in their houses — they little thought it would be so when they went into their beds; they did not in the least suspect, when the *doors of their ears* were unlocked, and the *windows of their eyes* were opened in the morning — to hear of such an *enemy's* invading the city, and that they Would see him, with such fury, enter the doors of their houses, break into every room, and look out of their windows with such a threatening countenance; as it is said in Lamentations 4:12, "All the world's inhabitants did not believe that an enemy or adversary could enter Jerusalem's gates!" Just so, the inhabitants of the city, would not have believed that the fire should have entered and prevailed to burn London to the ground!

That which made the ruin the more dismal, was, that it was begun on the Lord's day morning; never was there the like Sabbath in London; some churches were in flames that day; and God seems to come down, and to preach *himself* in them, as he did in Mount Sinai, when the Mount burned with fire! Such *warm preaching,* those churches never had! Such lightning dreadful sermons, never were before delivered in London.

In other churches ministers were preaching their farewell sermons, and people were hearing with quaking and astonishment! Instead of a holy rest, which Christians have taken on this day — there is a tumultuous hurrying about the streets towards the place that burned, and more tumultuous hurrying upon the spirits of those that sat still, and had only the notice of the ear, of the quick and strange spreading of the fire.

Now the police are up in arms, watching at every quarter for traitorous men, because of the general fears and jealousies, and rumors that fire-balls were thrown into houses by several of them, to help on and provoke the too furious flames. Now goods are hastily removed from the lower parts of the city; and the body of the people begin to flee, as the people did from the tabernacles of Korah, Dathan, and Abiram, when the earth split apart and swallowed them up! Numbers 16:27-32. Or rather as Lot fled from his house in Sodom, before it was consumed by fire from Heaven, Genesis 19. Yet some hopes were retained on the Lord's day, that the fire would be extinguished, especially by them who lived in the remote parts; they could scarcely imagine that the fire a mile off — should be able to reach *their* houses.

But the evening draws on, and now the fire is more visible and dreadful! Instead of the *black curtains of the night*, which used to be spread over the city, now the curtains are yellow! The *smoke* that arose from the burning parts, seemed like a *flame* in the night, which being blown upon the other parts by the wind, the whole city at some distance seemed to be on fire! Now hopes begin to sink, and a general consternation seizes upon the spirits of people. Little sleep is taken in London this night; the amazement, which the eye and ear effects upon the spirit, does either dry up, or drive away the sleep which used to bind up the senses. Some are at work to quench the fire with water, others endeavor to stop its course, by pulling down of houses; but all to no purpose. If the fire is a little allayed, or beaten down, or put to a stand in some places — it is but a very little while; it quickly recruits and recovers its force; it leaps and mounts, and makes the more furious onset! It drives back its opposers, snatches their weapons out of their hands, seizes upon the water-houses and engines, burns them, spoils them, and makes them unfit for service.

Some are upon their knees in the night, pouring out tears before the Lord, interceding for *poor London* in the day of its calamity; but alas, I fear there were too few *weeping Jeremiahs* at the throne of grace, too few *pleading Moses'* to stand in the gap; too few *wrestling Jacobs* to wrestle with the Lord, and hang about his arm. *London's sins* were too great, and *God's anger* against the city was too hot — to easily and presently to be quenched and allayed. And if by the intercession of some, a mitigation is obtained, so that the Lord does not stir up all his wrath, utterly to destroy the place as he did Sodom and Gomorrah; yet none can prevail to call back that wrath, and reverse that decree which is gone forth against the city! The time of London's fall has come; the fire has received its commission from God to burn down the city — and therefore all attempts to hinder it are in vain!

On that Sunday night, the fire had run as far as Thames Street; and had crept up into Cannon Street, and leveled it with the ground, and still is making forward by the water side, and upward to the brow of the hill, on which the city was built.

On Monday Grace-church Street is all in flames, with Lombard Street on the left hand, and part of Fen-church Street on the right, the fire working (though not so fast) against the wind that way. *Before* it were pleasant and stately houses, *behind* it were ruinous and desolate heaps. The burning then was in fashion of a *bow* — a dreadful bow it was, such as my eyes never before had seen; a bow which had God's arrow in it with a flaming point! It was a shining bow, which had fire in it, which signified God's anger, and his intention to destroy London with fire!

Now the flames break in upon Cornhill, that large and spacious street; and quickly cross the way by the trail of wood that lay in the streets, which had been pulled down from houses to prevent its spreading, and so the flames lick the whole street as they go; they mount up to the top of the highest houses; they descend down to the bottom of the lowest vaults and cellars; and march along on both sides of the way, with such a roaring noise, as never was heard in the city of London; no stately building so great as to resist their fury! The *Royal Exchange* itself, the glory of the merchants — is now invaded with much violence; and when once the fire was entered, how quickly did it run around the galleries, filling them with flames; then the fire descends the stairs, compasses the walks, giving forth flaming volleys, and filled the court with *sheets of fire*. By and by, down fall all the king's statues upon their faces, and the greatest part of the stone building after them, (the founder's statue only remaining) with such a noise, as was dreadful and astonishing!

Then, then the city did shake indeed, and the inhabitants did tremble, and flew away in great amazement from their houses, lest the flames should devour them! *Rattle, rattle, rattle!* was the noise which the fire struck upon the ear round about, as if there had been a thousand iron chariots beating upon the stones! And if you opened your eye to the the streets, where the fire had come — you would see in some places whole streets at once in flames, which issued forth as if they had been so many great forges protruding from the opposite windows, which folding together, were united into one great flame throughout the whole street, and then you might see the houses tumble, tumble, tumble, from one end of the street to the other with a great crash, leaving the foundations open to the view of the Heavens.

Now, fearfulness and terror surprises the citizens of London; confusion and astonishment falls upon them at this unheard of, unthought of judgment! It would have grieved the heart of an unconcerned person, to see the rueful looks, the pale cheeks, the tears trickling down from the eyes, (where the greatness of sorrow and amazement could give permission for such a vent,) the smiting of the breast; the wringing of the hands — to hear the sighs and groans, the doleful and weeping speeches of the distressed citizens, when they were bringing forth their wives, (some from their child-bed) and their little ones (some from their sick-bed) out of their houses, and sending them somewhere into the fields with their goods.

Now the *hopes* of London are gone, their *heart* is sunk; now there is a massive exodus from the city, and that in a greater hurry than before the plague; their goods being in greater danger by the fire, than their persons were by the sickness. Scarcely are some returned — but they must leave again, and not as before — now without any more hopes of ever returning, and living in those houses any more.

Now carts, and wagons, and coaches, and horses, as many as could have entrance into the city, were loaded; and any money is given for a cart, to bear forth into the fields some choice things, which were ready to be consumed! And some of the receiving countries had the audacity conscience to accept of the highest price, which the citizens did then offer in their extremity. I am mistaken if such money does not burn worse than the fire out of which it was raked.

Now casks of wine, and oil, and other commodities are tumbled along, and the owners shove as much of their goods as they can towards the gates. Everyone now becomes a porter to himself, and scarcely a back, either of man or woman — but had a burden on it in the street; it was very sad to see such throngs of poor citizens coming in and going forth from the unburnt parts, heavy loaded with some of their goods — but more heavy loaded with weighty grief and sorrow of heart, so that it is astonishing that they did not quite sink under these burdens.

*Monday* night was a dreadful night, when the wings of the night had shadowed the light of the Heavenly bodies; there was no darkness of night in London, for the fire shines now round about with a fearful blaze, which yielded such light in the streets as it had been the sun at noon-day!

Now the fire having wrought backward, strangely against the wind to Billings-gate, etc. along Thames Street eastward, runs up the hill to Tower Street, and having marched on from Grace-church Street, making further progress in Fen-church Street, and having spread its wing beyond Thames Street westward, mounts up from the water side through Dowgate, and Old Fish Street into Watling Street. But the great fury of the fire was in the broader streets; in the midst of the night it had come down Cornhill, and laid it in the dust; and runs along by the Stocks, and there meets with another fire, which came down Thread-needle Street; a little further with another, which came up from Wallbrook: a little further with another, which comes up from Bucklersbury; and all these four fires joining together, break into one bright flame at the corner of Cheapside, with such a dazzling light, and burning heat, and roaring noise by the fall of so many houses together, that was very amazing. And though it was somewhat stopped in its swift course at Mercers' Chapel — yet with great force in a while, it conquers the place, and burns through it, and then with great rage proceeds forward in Cheapside.

On *Tuesday* the fire was burning up the very heart of London! Cheapside is all in flames in a few hours time; many fires meeting there, as in the center; from Soper-lane, Bow-lane, Bread Street, and Friday Street — the fire comes up almost together, and breaks furiously into the Broad Street, and most of that side of the way was together in flames — a most dreadful spectacle! And then partly by the fire which came down by Mercers' Chapel, partly by the fall of the houses across the way — the other side is quickly kindled, and does not stand long after it.

Now the fire gets into Blackfriars, and so continues its course by the water, and makes up toward St. Paul's church, on that side, and the Cheapside fire besets the great building on this side, and the church, though all of stone outward, though naked of houses about it, and though so high above all buildings in the city — yet within a while, yields to the violent assaults of the conquering flames, and strangely takes fire at the top; now the lead melts and runs down, as if it had been *snow before the sun;* and the great beams and massive stones, fall on the pavement with a great noise, and great chunks of stone peel off strangely from the side of the walls.

The *conqueror* having got this high fort, darts its flames round about; now Paternoster-row, Newgate-market, the Old Bailey, and Ludgate-hill have submitted themselves to the devouring fire, which, with amazing speed rushes down the hill into Fleet Street. Now Cheapside fire marches along Iron-lane, Old Jury, Lawrence-lane, Milk Street, Wood Street, Gutter-lane, Foster-lane; now it runs along Lothbury, Cateaton Street, etc. From Newgate-market, it assaults Christ-church and conquers that great building, and burns through Martin's lane towards Aldersgate, and all about so furiously, as if it would not leave a house standing upon the ground!

Now horrible *flames of fire* mount up the sky, and the yellow smoke of London ascends up towards Heaven, like the smoke of a great furnace! It is a smoke so great, as darkened the sun at noon-day, (if at any time the sun peeped forth, it looked red like blood,) the cloud of smoke was so great, that travelers rode at noon-day some miles together in its shadow, though there were no other cloud beside to be seen in the sky.

And if Monday night was dreadful, *Tuesday* night was more dreadful, when far the greatest part of the city was consumed: many thousands who on Saturday had fine houses in the city, both for themselves, and to entertain others, now have not where to lay their head; and the fields are the only place which they can find for themselves and their goods; most of the late inhabitants of London lie all night in the open air, with no other canopy over them — but that of the Heavens.

The fire is still making towards them, and threatens the suburbs; it was amazing to see, how it had spread itself several miles in compass; and among other things that night, the sight of Guild-hall was a fearful spectacle, which stood the whole body of it together in view, for several hours together, after the fire had taken it, without flames, (I suppose because the timber was such solid oak) as if it had been a *palace of gold*, or a great building of burnished brass.

On *Wednesday* morning, when people expected that the suburbs would be burnt, as well as the city, and with speed were preparing their flight, as well as they could, with their luggage into the countries, and neighboring villages; then the Lord had pity on poor London; his heart is turned within him, and he "stays his rough wind in the day of the east wind;" his fury begins to be allayed: he has a remnant of people in London, and there shall a remnant of houses escape. The wind now is hushed; the commission of the fire is withdrawing, and it burns so gently, even where it meets with no opposition, that it was not hard to be quenched, in many places with a few hands.

Now the citizens begin to gather a little heart and encouragement in their endeavors to quench the fire. And when once the fire was gotten under control, it was kept under control, and on Thursday the flames were extinguished.

But on Wednesday night, when the people late of *London*, now of the *fields* — hoped to get a little rest on the ground, where they had spread their beds, a more dreadful fear falls upon them than they had before, through a rumor that the French were coming armed against them to cut their throats, and rob them of what they had saved out of the fire; they were now naked and weak, and in an ill-condition to defend themselves, and the hearts, especially of the females, do quake and tremble, and are ready to die within them! Yet many citizens having lost their houses, and almost all that they had, are fired with rage and fury; and they begin to stir up themselves like lions, or like bears bereaved of their whelps, and now *"Arms, arms, arms!"* resounds the fields and suburbs with a great noise. We may guess at the distress and perplexity of the people this night, which was something alleviated when the falseness of the alarm was perceived.

Thus fell great London, that ancient city! that populous city! London! which was the queen city of the land, and as famous as most cities in the world; none so famous for the gospel and zealous profession of the reformed religion. And yet, how is London departed like smoke, and her glory laid in the dust! How is her destruction come, which no man thought of, and her desolation in a moment! How do the nations gaze and wonder! How does the whole land tremble at the noise of her fall! How do her citizens droop and hang down their heads; her women and virgins weep, and sit in the dust! Oh, the paleness that now sits upon the cheeks! the astonishment and confusion that covers the face, the dismal apprehensions that arise in the minds of most concerning the dreadful consequences which are likely to be of this fall of London!

How is . . .

the *pride* of London stained,  
her *beauty* spoiled,  
her *arm* broken,  
her *strength* departed,

her *riches* almost gone,
her *treasures* so much consumed!

The head now is sick, and the whole body faint; the heart is wounded, and every other part is sensible of its stroke! Never was England in greater danger of being made a prey to a foreign power, than since the firing and fall of this city, which had the strength and treasure of the nation in it. How is London destroyed, that rich city! that joyous city! One corner indeed is left; but more than as many houses as were within the walls, are turned into ashes!

The merchants now have left the Royal Exchange; the buyers and sellers have now forsaken the streets: Grace-church Street, Cornhill, Cheapside, Newgate-market, and the like places, which used to have throngs of traffickers — now are empty of inhabitants; and instead of the stately houses which stood there last summer, now they lie this winter in ruinous heaps of ashes! The glory of London is now fled away like a bird, the trade of London is shattered and broken to pieces, her delights also are vanished, and pleasant things laid waste: now no singing to the sound of the violin, and dancing to the sweet music of other instruments; now no drinking wine in bowls, and stretching upon the beds of lust; now no excess of wine and banquettings; no feasts in halls and sumptuous dishes; no amorous looks, and wanton dalliances; no ruffling silks, and costly dresses; these things are all at an end.

But if houses for sin alone were sunk, and fuel for lust alone were consumed, it would not be so much: but the houses also for God's worship, (which formerly were a bulwark against the fire; partly through the *walls* about them, partly through the *fervent prayers* within them,) now are devoured by the flames, and the habitations of many who truly fear God, have not escaped! And in the places where God has been served, and his servants have lived — now nettles are growing, owls are screeching, thieves and cut-throats are lurking: a sad face there is now in the ruinous part of London, and *terrible the voice of the Lord* has been — which has been crying, yes, roaring in the city by these dreadful judgments of the plague and fire, which *he* has brought upon us!

Thus you have the narration of the plague and fire *judgments* themselves.

# Section 7

## Concerning the CAUSE of these judgments. WHY has the Lord spoken by such terrible things in the city of London?

In giving an account hereof, I shall make use of the second Doctrine observed from the words: That when God speaks most terribly — he answers most righteously.

They are *God's* judgments, and therefore they must needs be *righteous* judgments. Can there be unrighteousness in God? No, impossible; for how then could he be God? How then "could he judge the world? Let God be true, and every man a liar," Romans 3:5, 6. Let God be righteous, and all the world unrighteous; for *light* may more easily depart from the sun, and *heat* be separated from the fire, and the whole creation may more easily drop into nothing — than God cease to be just and righteous, in the severest judgments which he inflicts upon the children of men.

If any profane mockers do reply against God, and reflect upon his righteousness and goodness towards his own people, because these judgments have fallen so sore upon London, the glory of the land, yes, of the world; for the number of *holy people* (as in scoff they call them) which dwell in it: if God were so righteous and favorable to the godly — would he bend his bow and shoot so many arrows among them as he did in the visitation by the plague — while he allowed so many notoriously wicked people to escape? Would he send the fire to consume so many habitations of the godly — while the houses of the most wicked and vile were preserved? I shall labor to stop the mouths of such who are ready to open them against the King of Heaven, by proposing to consideration these following particulars.

1. "That God's way is sometimes in the sea, and his paths in the great waters; and his footsteps are not known!" "That his judgments are unsearchable, and his ways past finding out," Romans 11:33. And that even then "he is righteous in all his ways, and holy in all his works," Psalm 145:17. "And when clouds and darkness are round about him, righteousness and judgment are the habitation of his throne," Psalm 97:2. And when "his judgments

are a great deep, his righteousness is like the great mountains," Psalm 36:6.

We do not understand all the mysteries of *nature*, neither are we acquainted with all the mysteries of *state*; and if there are some mysteries in *God's* way of governing the world, and distributing temporal mercies and judgments, which we do not apprehend in everything the meaning of, and cannot so fully trace God's righteousness and goodness therein — it is because our *eyes* are shut, and that we are covered with darkness! Therefore let us shut our *mouths* too, and seal up our lips with silence, not daring in the least to utter anything which may derogate from these attributes in God, which are as inviolable and unchangeable as his very being.

2. But secondly, the reason of God's judgments and righteousness therein, with the salve of his goodness towards his own people, may be apprehended, if we consider,

First, that these judgments of plague and fire, are both of them *national* judgments.

1. The judgment of the plague was *national*; inasmuch as London was the chief city; inasmuch as the King's court was here, and most countries had relations here: and all countries had concernments here: moreover the plague was not only in London and Westminster, and places near adjacent; but it was dispersed into the counties at a farther distance, as Cambridge, Norwich, Colchester, and other towns, where it raged either the same in the next year, as much proportionably as it did in London.

2. The judgment of the fire, which burned down only the City, and left Westminster and the suburbs standing, and did not reach into the countries — yet was a national judgment, because London was the metropolis of the land; because the beauty, riches, strength, and glory of the whole kingdom lay in London; and it was not the inhabitants of the city who alone did suffer by this fire — but the whole land, more or less, do and will feel the smart hereof.

Secondly, These judgments then being national, it is not unreasonable to say, that *national sins have been the cause of them*; and if so, we may readily find a reason of God's righteousness in these proceedings, when the sins of the land are so obvious and so heinous. He is a great stranger in England — who does not know how wickedness has abounded in these later years! His eyes must be fast shut — who does not see what a deluge of profaneness and impiety has broken in like a mighty torrent, and overflowed the land — who has not taken notice of those barefaced villainies which have been committed among us, which is a great question whether any ages before us could parallel. We read in Scripture of Sodom and Gomorrah, and the wickedness of Jerusalem; secular histories make mention of Rome, Venice, Naples, Paris, and other places very wicked.

But who can equal *England*, which calls itself Christian and Protestant, for such desperate and audacious affronts and indignities which have been offered to the divine Majesty by the gallants (as they are called) of our times? How was Hell, as it were, broke loose; and how were men worse than those which, in our Savior's time, were possessed with devils, who cut themselves with stones, and tore their own flesh; even such who went about like so many Hell-hounds and incarnate devils, cursing, swearing and blaspheming, inventing new oaths, and glorying therein, delighting to tear the name of God, and to spit forth their rancour and malice in his very face?

And can we then be at a loss for a reason of God's righteousness in his thus punishing England, by beginning thus furiously with London? When were there so many atheists about London, and in the land, who denied the very being of God; when so many gentlemen (who looked upon it as one piece of their breeding to cast off all sentiments of a Deity) did walk our streets, and no arguments would work them to a persuasion of the truth of God's being, shall we wonder, if the Lord appears in a terrible way, that he might be known by the judgments which he executes?

When so many denied the Divine authority of the Scriptures, the very foundation of our Christian faith, and reckoned themselves, by their principles, among Turks, Pagans, and other infidels, however, they called themselves Christians, and hereby put such an affront upon the Lord Jesus Christ, the only Son of the Most High God — is it strange that the Lord should speak so terribly, to show his indignation? When there was such blowing at, and endeavors to put out that light which would show men the way to Heaven; such hatred and opposition against the power of godliness; when the name of a *saint* was matter of derision and scorn; when there was such *wallowing in filthy fornication and adultery*, in swinish drunkenness and intemperance; when such oppression, bribery, such malice, cruelty, such unheard of wickedness, and hideous impiety, grown to such a height in the land — may we not reasonably think that such people as were thus guilty, being in the ship, were a great cause of the storm of God's anger, which has made such a shipwreck?

The *plague* indeed, when it was come, made little discrimination between the *bodies* of the righteous and the bodies of the wicked. Even when converted, the body remains as it was, as frail, and weak, and exposed to diseases and death, as before, and as the body of any wicked person; and therefore the infectious disease of the plague coming into a populous city, the bodies of the righteous, among the rest, receive the contagion, and they fall in the *common calamity.* Yet there is a difference in the manner of their death, and a difference in their place and state after death, as has been spoken of before — but the kind of death is the same.

So the fire makes no discrimination between the *houses* of the godly, and the houses of the ungodly; they are all made of the same combustible matter, and are enkindled one by another.

Indeed the godly have God to be their eternal habitation, and they are citizens of the New Jerusalem, which is above; a city which has foundations, whose builder and maker is God; an abiding city, which the fire cannot reach; and their persons are secured from the flames of eternal fire in Hell. But they have no promise nor security for the preservation of their houses from fire here in this world. The judgments of the plague and fire being sent, work according to their nature, without distinguishing the righteous.

But if we further inquire into the reason, Why the **plague** was sent the last year, and such a plague as has not been known these forty years; which raged so sorely, when there was no such sultriness of weather (as in other years) to increase it; and why the **fire** was sent this year, and such a fire as neither we, nor our forefathers ever knew, neither do we read of in any history of any so great in any place? What shall we say was the *cause* of these extraordinary national judgments — but the extraordinary national *sins!*

It was an extraordinary hand of God which brought the *plague,* of which no natural cause can be assigned why it should be so great that year more than in former years — but that sin was grown to greater height! And that a *fire* should prevail against all attempts to quench it, to burn down the city, and that judgment just following upon the heels of the other; what reason can be assigned — but that England's sins, and God's displeasure have been extraordinary! God is a God of patience, and it is not a small thing which will move him; he is slow to anger, it must needs be then some *great provocation* which makes him so furious. He is highly offended — before he lifts up his hand; and he is exceedingly incensed — before his anger breaks forth into such a flame.

For my part, I truly think, if it had not been for the *crying abominations of the times*, which are not chiefly to be limited to the city of London. And if the means of God's prescription, according to the rule of his Word, had by England been made use of — that both plague and fire had been prevented.

Thirdly, moreover, it may be said that some *particular people*, by some more peculiar and notorious sins in the city, may have provoked the Lord to bring punishment upon the whole place, if the land were not so generally profane and wicked. May a whole city may be punished for the wickedness of one man? Yes, we read of David, though so good a man — yet when he numbered the people (a small sin in comparison with the sins of some others in our days) God was provoked to send such a dreadful plague, not on himself — but upon his people, that there died 70,000 men by it in three days; and David said, "I have sinned and done wickedly; but these *sheep* — what have they done?" 2 Sam. 24:10, 18.

Fourthly, If it be inquired how God's mercy to his people appears — when these judgments have fallen so heavy upon many of them? I answer,

1. Those of God's own people who have fallen by the *plague*, are received to greater grace and mercy in Heaven, than they were capable of here on earth; and they are moreover delivered from evil to come, which has since, and may further come upon us.

2. Those whose houses have fallen by the *fire*, the Lord could, and confident I am, the Lord has made them greater gainers another way: they have lost, it may be, much in *temporal* things; but they are gainers of *spiritual* things, which are of a higher and more excellent nature. I have known and heard of many of God's people whose houses are burnt and goods spoiled, who have taken the loss with so much cheerfulness, humility, meekness, patience, contentment, and thankfulness, that anything was saved, if it were only their lives, that it has been my wonder and joy. To gain such a spirit, has more of good, than the loss of all external enjoyments has of evil!

3. Further, If these judgments have fallen upon God's people — we must know that they have their sins, which have deserved them. Possibly some have begun to comply with the wicked in their wicked ways. It may be, that they had . . .

grown more loose in their walking,
and formal in the service of God,
and their hearts more set on the world.

The sins of God's people have more heinous aggravations than the sins of the wicked, being committed against . . .

clearer light,
dearer love,
sweeter mercies, and
stronger obligations;

and therefore provoke God the more to wrath. Hence He threatens His own people, especially, to punish them when they transgress, "You only have I known of all the families of the earth — and therefore I will punish you for your iniquities." Amos 3:2

Besides, God's people have need of awakening judgments . . .

to arouse them,
to humble them for sin, and
to loosen and wean them from the world!

It is in love and faithfulness, that God inflicts such judgments upon them.

"Before I was afflicted I went astray — but now I obey Your Word." Psalm 119:67

"It was good for me to be afflicted — so that I might learn Your decrees." Psalm 119:71

"I know, O Lord, that Your laws are righteous, and in faithfulness You have afflicted me." Psalm 119:75

4. We must remember that it is God's usual course to begin with his own house, 1 Peter 4:17. "Judgment begins at the house of God."

Fifthly, To conclude, Do any of the ungodly question God's righteousness, because in these common calamities, they have hitherto survived and escaped?

1. It is but an ill requital, and ill use which they make of God's *patience* and *goodness*, which he has exercised towards them, that hereby he might lead them unto repentance, Romans 2:4, 5.

2. Let them stay awhile, and God himself will answer them, and give them an *experimental conviction* of his righteous judgments, 1 Peter 4:17, 18. "If judgment begins at the house of God — then what shall the end be of those who obey not the Gospel? And if the righteous are scarcely be saved — where shall the ungodly and sinners appear?" We read in Psalm 75:8, "The Lord holds a cup in his hand that is full of foaming wine mixed with spices. He pours out the wine in judgment, and all the wicked must drink it, draining it to the dregs!" He may give *his people* to drink the *top* of

it; but the most bitter and dreggish part, which is at the bottom — the wicked shall drink and drain in Hell! If God whips his children with rods — he will scourge his enemies with scorpions!

I am persuaded that the notoriously ungodly of this generation, will not go out of this world without some remarkable temporal judgment; and that the Lord will make them feel something even here. The wicked will feel what an evil and a bitter thing it is so audaciously to fly in the face of the great God, by their hideous oaths and blasphemies, by their horrid wickedness and abominations, whereby they do, as it were, challenge God to do His worst against them!

And when God draws forth His glittering sword, and makes ready His sharp arrow upon the string; when God clothes Himself with fury as with a garment, and His hand takes hold on vengeance; when their iniquities are grown fully ripe, and the day of their visitation and recompense has come — how then will the wicked be terrified? What amazing terror will there then surprise this vile generation? "Can their hearts endure, or their hands be strong — in the day that the Lord shall deal with them?" Ezekiel 22:14. Then the Lord will roar from His holy habitation with such a terrible voice, as shall make their ears to tingle, their hearts to quake and tremble! He will roar like a lion, and tear them in pieces, when there shall be none to deliver!

If the shaking of his rod has moved them, and the beginning of his judgments, which he has executed upon others, has affrighted them, what will their behavior be when the scourge is laid upon their own backs, and judgment shall fall upon their own heads! Surely the judgments intended purposely for the ungodly, are yet to come! Surely the judgments intended purposely for the ungodly, are yet to come! And they will be exceeding great, because of the more pure and unmixed wrath which will accompany them!

Just so, they are likely to be very near, because they are filling up the measure of their wickedness so fast, and they seem to be arrived even to the uttermost of sin; surely their judgment neither lingers nor slumbers — but is upon the wing, *hastening* towards them; surely the arm of the Lord is awakened, and lifted up on high; and though infinite patience holds it up a little while, to try whether the judgments already executed upon others, before their eyes will work any good effect upon them, so as to awaken them and stop them, and turn them from their evil ways. Yet, if they proceed in their sinful course, God's arm, I am persuaded, will come down with such force and fury upon them, that their destruction shall be remarkable to all that are round about them!

And I am much of that persuasion, that the Lord will, as it were, hang up many of the villains of our times, who have been guilty of such treachery and rebellion against the great King of Heaven — as it were in chains, and make their punishment here as notorious as their sins have been, that the whole world may hear and fear, and take heed of such vile practices!

I suppose they may not now expect judgment, nor fear it — any more than the whole world did their drowning in Noah's day; or Sodom and Gomorrah did their burning — because *deceitful sin* has hardened their hearts! Long continuance in sin, with impunity, has seared their consciences as with a hot iron; but then they are in the greatest danger, when they sleep with the greatest security! When men grow desperately hardened against often and all reproofs, by Word and rod too, what follows but sudden destruction, and that without remedy! Proverbs 29:1. "And when men cry *'peace and safety'* — then sudden destruction comes upon them, as travail upon a woman with child — and they shall not escape!" 1 Thessalonians 5:3

And if some of this perverse and wicked generation drop away without a remarkable *temporal* destruction, God will make his righteousness evident to them in the eternal world — when he claps up their souls as prisoners in the lowest dungeon of Hell, appointing horrid devils to be their jailors, flames of fire to be their clothing, hideous terrors and woe to be their food; Cain, Judas, and other damned tormented spirits to be their companions, where they must lie bound in the chains of darkness, until the judgment of the great day!

And when that fearful day has finally come, and the angels have blown the last trumpet, and gathered the elect to the right hand of Christ — then one will be sent with the keys of the bottomless pit, and the infernal prison will be opened for a while; and like so many rogues in chains — they shall, together with all their fellow sinners, be brought forth, and be joined to the dirty flesh of their bodies, which, like a nasty rag, they shall then put on; and with most rueful looks, and trembling joints, and horrible shrieks, and inexpressible confusion and terror — they shall behold the Lord Jesus Christ, whom in their life-time they despised and affronted — come down from Heaven in flaming fire, to take vengeance upon them! He Himself will sentence them to the flames of eternal fire, and drive them away from His throne and presence — into the utter darkness of Hell, where they must take up their lodging for evermore!

Then, then there will be a clear revelation of the righteous and dreadful judgments of this great God unto the world, and upon this accursed generation.

But more fully to clear up the reason of London's judgments, and the righteousness of God herein — God has, indeed, spoken very terribly — but he has answered us very righteously. London was not so godly, as some speak by way of scoff. No! if London had been more generally godly, and more powerfully godly — then these judgments might have been escaped, and the ruin of the city prevented!

No! it was the ungodliness of London — which brought the plague and fire upon London. There was a general *plague* upon the *heart*, a more dangerous infection, and deadly plague of *sin* — before there was sent a plague upon the body! There was a *fire* of manifold lusts which was enkindled, and burned in the bosom — sometimes issuing out flames at the *door of the mouth*, and at the *windows of the eyes* of the inhabitants, before the fire was kindled in the city, which swallowed up so many habitations.

We have fallen (thousands of people) into the grave by the plague; thousands of houses, as a great monument upon them, by the fire! And *WHY* is it? "Your sins have been your downfall!" Hosea 14:1. "The crown is fallen from our heads!" And what is the reason? "because we have sinned against the Lord," Lam. 5:16. God has spoken terribly — but he has answered righteously. As he gives great and especial *mercies*, in answer unto prayer — so he sends great and extraordinary *judgments*, in answer unto sin! There is a voice and loud cry, especially in some sins, which "enters into the ears of the Lord Almighty!" James 5:4. When God speaks by terrible things — he makes but a righteous return to this cry.

And though these judgments of plague and fire are national judgments, and may be the product of national sins — I truly am persuaded, that God was more highly provoked by some who dwelt outside of the city, than with those which dwelt in it. I mean the profane and ungodly generation, who chiefly live more remotely; and that God, being so provoked, was the more ready to strike, and let his hand fall so heavy upon London. Yet, since many of the ungodly crew were gotten into the city itself; and most in the city, who were not of them, and did not dare to commit their impieties — yet made themselves guilty, by not mourning for them; and since London itself has been guilty of so many crying sins (as I shall endeavor to show), God's righteousness in the *terrible things of London* will be evident, especially if we consider,

1. That God has punished London *no more* than their iniquities have deserved.

2. That God has punished London *less* than their iniquities have deserved.

**1. God has punished London *no more* than their iniquities deserved.** Great sins deserve great plagues — and have not the sins of London been great? Let us make an inquiry after London's sins.

Here I shall offer some sins for consideration, and let London judge whether she is not guilty, and whether the Lord has not been *plaguing* her, and *burning* her, and possibly, yes, probably, will bring utter ruin and desolation upon her — unless she sees, and mourns, and turns soon!

It is out of dear and tender love to London (with whom I would willingly live and die) that I write these things to put them in mind of their sins — that they might take some speedy course for a turning away the fierce anger of the Lord which is kindled against them for sin, lest he next proceed to bring *utter ruin* upon them! Surely they have not more reason to think that God's anger is turned away since the *fire* — than they had to think it was turned away after the *plague*. But rather they may conclude, that though the *fire* of the city is quenched — yet the fire of God's anger still burns more dreadfully than the other fire, and that his hand is stretched out still to destroy! Therefore, O all you inhabitants about London! open your eyes, and ears, and hearts, and allow a word of reproof for your sins!

Do not deal with this catalogue of your sins, as *Jehoiachim* did with *Jeremiah's scroll*, who burnt it in the fire, not being able to bear his words. But do with it as *John* did with his *little book* — eat it, and digest it; though it is bitter in the mouth, as well as in the belly — it is bitter medicine — but necessary for the preservation of a sick, languishing city, which is even ready to be destroyed.

And here I shall begin with more *gospel sins*, which, though natural, conscience is not so ready to accuse of — yet in the account of God are the *most heinous sins*. And I would have a regard not only to recent — but to *former* sins, which, possibly, may now be more out of view, and forgotten, and which some may be hardened in, because the guilty have not been so particularly and sensibly punished, (though God's *sparing* of them, has been in order to their *repentance*) or their punishments in some kind has been accounted by them no punishments; or their punishments have been mistaken, and their hearts have swelled against the *instruments* made use of by God therein, instead of accepting of the punishment of their iniquity, and humbling themselves deeply before the Lord.

I say, I would call to remembrance *former* sins, as well as recent sins, which are more visible now, and apparent; for as God, being so slow to anger, has not been quickly moved to such indignation; but, as we have reason to think, that *his wrath has been a long time boiling in his breast* — before it was raised to this height as to *boil over*, and pour down plague and fire upon the city of London; so we may reasonably infer, that sins committed by London long ago, were the fuel put under, which caused this *boiling of his anger*; which, because other milder judgments have not wrought the kindly effect of repentance — the Lord has been provoked to express his wrath in this way, which has been more feeling and dreadful.

Moreover, when I reckon up London's sins, I would not reflect alone upon any one party, inasmuch as all parties have sinned; and I believe the Lord has been offended with all, as in his judgments — he has made no difference; that all might be awakened to see their faults with sorrow and shame.

And if it were fit, I would begin here with *myself*, being persuaded that *my sins*, more than thousands of others, have helped to fill up the vial of God's anger! But as I go along, I shall endeavor, by the grace of God, to apply to myself the sins which conscience will accuse of, that I may bewail and amend. And I will beseech every one of you who cast your eyes upon these lines — to do the like, and to compare them with those lines which are written in the *book of your consciences*. And where you find a transcript — read and read again; consider and lay to heart; get to your knees, confess, and labor to drop at least some *tears* into the bottle; which, if this little book might help gather from your eyes, and you could be persuaded to pour forth such waters before the Lord, they might help to quench the violence of the fire of God's anger, which we have reason to fear is still burning against us!

# Section 8

## A CATALOGUE of London's Sins, which have provoked the Lord to speak with so terrible a Voice in the City.

1. The first sin of London, is **slighting of the Gospel**. The Gospel in England has for more than a hundred years, shined forth out of the clouds of *Popery* and *Heathenism* — which once overspread the land. And in no place of England has the Gospel been preached with greater power and purity, than in London. And what *reception* has it found? has it been *valued* according to its worth and excellency; has it been *received* as if it had come down from the God of Heaven, expressing his love and good-will towards the children of men, as if it had brought such good news and glad tidings, as salvation by Jesus Christ?

Read the eulogy which the Apostle Peter gives of the *salvation* made known by the Gospel, "Concerning this salvation, the prophets, who spoke of the grace that was to come to you, searched intently and with the greatest care, trying to find out the time and circumstances to which the Spirit of Christ in them was pointing when he predicted the sufferings of Christ and the glories that would follow. It was revealed to them that they were not serving themselves but you, when they spoke of the things that have now been told you by those who have preached the gospel to you by the Holy Spirit sent from Heaven. Even angels long to look into these things!" 1 Peter 1:10-12

The prophets of old did inquire and search — but did not so clearly understand the Gospel, as now it is revealed. Our Savior tells his disciples, that "many prophets and kings have desired to *see* the things which they saw, and had not seen them; and to *hear* the things which they did hear, and had not heard them; for indeed this mystery was hidden from ages and generations, which God then made manifest unto the saints," Luke 10:24, Colossians 1:26.

And the Apostle Paul tells us, that "though the ministration of the law were glorious, insomuch that it made the face of Moses to shine," unto whom the law was revealed upon the Mount, "yet that it had no glory — in *comparison* with the ministration of the Gospel, whose glory did so far excel," 2 Corinthians 3:7-10. The mysteries of God's wisdom and love revealed in the Gospel, being so glorious, surely are worthy of acceptance and esteem, especially when the angels, who are not so much personally concerned, desire to look into these things, unto whom it is said, "Is made known by the church, the manifold wisdom of God." Ephesians 3:10

And yet these *great* things, which have been reported by those who have preached the Gospel, with the Holy Spirit sent down from Heaven, have been *undervalued* in London. The Gospel has been *slighted* in London; and though some have been more notoriously guilty — yet who can altogether excuse themselves from this sin? Now that the conviction may be more full — I shall charge the sin more *particularly*.

1. The **ignorant** people in London have been guilty of this sin. The light of the Gospel has shined about them — but they have muffled up themselves in darkness, and allowed Satan to keep them hood-winked, lest the light of the glorious Gospel should enter, and lead them out of his snare! Thousands in the city have been *willfully ignorant* — though they have had means of knowledge, so near, and so easy to come by! Multitudes of the ignorant have already perished from London — and multitudes still remain in their ignorance. O the neglect that there has been of learning catechisms! and how few have endeavored to acquaint themselves with the principles of the Christian religion — that they might have the more full and clear understanding of the Gospel?

2. The **wicked** and **profane** have been guilty of slighting the Gospel. How many such people have there crowded, and are still rushing out of London into Hell, when the light of the Gospel shined upon them, which would have guided them in the way to Heaven! Because this light has been too *troublesome* in its discovery, and *reproof* of their dear and sweet sins — they have hated it, and endeavored to fly as far as they could from it, or to *shut their eyes* as hard as they could against it!

3. The **moral** people also have been guilty; there have been many sober citizens and matrons, moral youths and virgins, who have been free from the gross pollutions which are in the world through lust; who have been diligent in their calling, just in their dealings, courteous, and sweet-natured in their demeanor — and yet without the least degree of the power of godliness, without which it is impossible they should be saved!

Alas! none of these have given any warm welcome unto the Gospel in their hearts, which has been so long preached in the city. The kindness of a *friend* has been esteemed by them; but the kindness of *God* has not been regarded. If a messenger had come and told them how they might save their estates, when in danger of loss, or how to save their relations when in danger of death — O how welcome would such a messenger and tidings have been! But when ministers have preached the Gospel unto them, which tells them how they should save their souls, which are in danger of death and Hell — such tidings have had no relish with them! They act as if they had no souls, or were in no danger!

The *light* has shined before them — but there has been a *cloud* in their eye, they could not discern it; or they have looked upon it afar off, they have not drawn near, and brought it home, nor considered it in their hearts — that they might order themselves, according to its guidance and direction.

4. The **hypocrites** have been guilty of this sin; these have drawn nearer to this light, than any of the former; so near, that they have seemed to be clothed with its beams, they have lighted their lamps hereby, and have shined forth in a glorious blaze of an *outward profession*. Yet there has been, even in these, an *inward secret disrelish* of the Gospel, especially of some things in it: there have been some *secret rooms* in their hearts, into which they would not allow the light to enter, lest it should unveil those *beloved Delilahs* — which there, they have nourished and brought up!

They have been rotten at the *core*, and have had some unmortified lust within, which the world has not taken notice of; so that if the Gospel has been received by them — it has been only in the outward form, not in the *inward power*. If the light has been received — it has been without its heat and life. Hence it has come to pass, that some of these hypocrites, who seemed to be stars of the first magnitude — have proved only *blazing stars* and *comets*, which in a short time have fallen and sunk into worldliness, or fearful apostasy.

5. The **erroneous** have been guilty of this sin. Some, and not a few, in London, under this glorious sunshine of the Gospel, which has come from Heaven — have lighted a candle at the fire of Hell, and labored to set it up in opposition to the true light of the Gospel, crying out, "New light, new light!" Satan himself has appeared in London like an angel of light, and employed his emissaries and wicked instruments (who have seemed to be *ministers of righteousness* — but have had a *wolfish ravenous heart* under the dress and clothing of the sheep) to vent many damnable and destruc-

tive opinions in our church, under pretense of *new discoveries* and revelations of the Spirit; and through this false candle-light, could never abide the test, and put forth any beams of convincing truth; but darkened and disappeared upon the approach of the sun, where it shined in its power.

Yet too many whose eyes were too sore to look upon the glorious beams of the sun, and yet withal their hearts too fearful to remain wholly in the dark, without any show of light — withdrew themselves from the former, and sought after the latter in dark corners, where alone such *rotten wood* could seem to shine, and such *candles* could give forth any light; and choosing *night* rather than day, they followed these false wandering fires, though they were led by them into many a precipice.

It is sad to remember, and seriously to consider — what *errors* and *strong delusions* have abounded and prevailed in our Gospel days. How many false teachers have there been among us, which have crept in unawares; how many *Jesuits* and *Priests* sent from Rome and other places, to rend and tear our Protestant church to pieces, that they might make way for the introduction of popery; at least to cast a disgrace upon Protestantism, and delude many of us with the opinions they have broached, and to confirm their own people in their delusions.

Thus many cunning and learned *Jesuits* have disguised themselves in the habit of tailors, shoemakers, and of other mechanical tradesmen, that they might seem to the people to have been taught those things by the Spirit, which have been the product of much study. Thus these cursed villains, "of old ordained to condemnation, have privily brought in damnable heresies," putting themselves into any shapes, that they might mislead, and the better "lie in wait to deceive" poor souls. Some "denying the *Lord* that bought them;" others denying the foundation, undermining the divine authority of the *Scriptures*; others laboring to overthrow the doctrine of *justification*, and striking at most fundamental doctrines of the Christian faith. And all of them endeavoring to undermine the ministry of Christ's institution and sending, calling them Anti-christian, Baal's Priests, false prophets, doing what they could to bring them and their ministry out of esteem — that they might the more effectually prevail with the people to receive their false doctrines, and arm them hereby against gospel truth; and sweetening their poison with "good words, and fair speeches — they have deceived the hearts of the simple, so that many did follow their pernicious ways, by reason of whom the way of truth has been evil spoken of!" And whatever *good* words they had, they were but "*feigned* words, whereby they made merchandise of souls, whose judgment now a long time lingers not," and whose damnation slumbers not!" 2 Peter 2:1-3

These the Apostle calls them "spots and blemishes, sporting themselves with their own deceivings; wells without water; clouds carried about with a tempest; raging waves of the sea, foaming out their own shame; wandering stars, unto whom is reserved blackness of darkness forever!" 2 Peter 2:13-17; Jude 15.

And yet many of these were hearkened unto, and adhered unto, by too many in London, rather than the true Gospel ministers, commissioned by the Lord Jesus Christ himself, and ordained according to the prescription of his Word.

Now all these people have been *slighters* of the Gospel of Jesus Christ, the ignorant, the profane, the hypocrite, and the erroneous; and if you place them all in one company, how few will there remain in London, that have sincerely and heartily embraced the truth as it is in Jesus, and upon whom the Gospel has made a powerful and saving impression!

And even among those who have been affected and converted by the preaching of the Gospel, and had greatly esteemed it at first hearing and believing; how was their esteem of the Gospel fallen, and their affection cooled! Did not Gospel-ordinances begin to lose their worth and excellency, and grow tedious and wearisome unto them?

O, how generally unthankful was London for Gospel privileges and liberties! Yes, many began to be very particular and wanton, and the Gospel was not relished, unless it were served up with such cleverness and dressings, in which some ministers possibly did too much endeavor to please themselves and the people; and then the *sauce* was more relished than the *food* itself, and the appetite of many was so spoiled — that plain, wholesome, soul-saving truths, would not go down with them!

Londoners began to be glutted with the Gospel; and like the Israelites in the wilderness, their souls began to loath the manna which came down from Heaven. A strange curiosity there was in spiritual palates; which in many turned to a *loathing of the food*, insomuch that the Gospel became a burden unto them, and thence it was that "The time will come when men will not put up with sound doctrine. Instead, to suit their own desires, they will gather around them a great number of teachers to say what their itching ears want to hear. They will turn their ears away from the truth and turn aside to myths!" 2 Tim. 4:3, 4.

And those who continued steadfast in the truth, did not duly *prize* the Gospel, none of them according to its dignity and worth. No wonder then if God grows angry at such *contempts* and *affronts* as were hereby offered unto him, and withdraws the food so much, which they grew so weary of! No wonder that he allows so many of their teachers to be thrust into corners, and so much withdraws the beams of that light which was so much abused. And when they are not sensible of his displeasure in this — no wonder if he sends the plague and fire, to awaken them unto a sensibility!

When the "King sent forth his servants to call the guests to the wedding-feast — and they make light of it, and excused themselves, and went away, one to his farm, another to his merchandise — and the rest seized his servants, mistreated them and killed them — the king was angry, and sent forth his armies to destroy those murderers, and burned their city!" Matthew 22:1-8.

Just so, God has sent forth his *servants* to call Londoners to this feast; how many invitations have they had to come unto Christ, to receive him to save them, and to feed upon him, from whom alone they can get any spiritual nourishment. But how many in London have had their *excuses*; they have been following their merchandise and other business, and could not come. And what poor treatment his servants have had — the Lord knows. I do not say that London has treated them despitefully, and slain them; but has not their message been slighted by London? And is it a wonder then, if the king who sent them is angry, and sends a fire to burn down the city?

No greater *favor* could be showed, no greater *privilege* could be enjoyed — than to have the Gospel powerfully preached, and ordinances purely administered; but has it been generally so accounted in London? Has not merchandise, and thriving in the world, (which yet they have not thrived in) been preferred before this, by many thousands in the city? When God has been at such an expense to work out a way for man's salvation; when he has revealed such wonders of astonishing love in sending his only begotten Son out of Heaven to clothe himself in our flesh, that therein he might purchase life and salvation for us who were sunk so low from our primitive state by sin, and were exposed to death and eternal wrath, and unavoidable endless misery in Hell; and has sent his ambassadors of peace to bring unto us the glad tidings hereof, and in his name to make known the way, the author, the terms: and to entreat us that we would accept of life and reconciliation to God, who without any injury to himself could ruin us everlastingly, and get himself a name thereby. And yet, when the Gospel is preached, that we should *undervalue* and *slight* both messenger and message; surely this has been an affront unto the Lord, who has sent his ambassadors on this errand, and carries with it such *ingratitude* as cannot be paralleled!

No doubt, but this *sin of slighting the Gospel* is a prime sin, which has provoked God against London, to come forth in such fury; and if London does not repent before long, and labor to recover its relish and esteem of the Gospel, and make more evident demonstrations of it — I fear that the Lord will quite remove the Gospel from them; and then nothing is likely to follow but *desolation* and *woe*. God does not *remove his glory* at once — but by steps; first, "the glory of the Lord departs from the inner court, to the threshold of the house," Ezekiel 10:3, 4; "from the threshold of the house to the door of the east-gate," verses 18, 19, "then it goes from the midst of the city, and stands upon the mountain," chapter 11:23.

The Gospel is the glory of London, and has the glory of the Lord made none of these removes? Is it not come forth of the inner court? Has it not left the threshold? Is not a departing of it quite from the city threatened? Will anything recover it, if we do not recover our appetite, and prize, and cry after it?

If the Gospel goes — God will go; the Gospel being the sign and means of his special presence; and "woe be unto us when God shall depart from us!" Hos. 9:12. And if God departs with the Gospel — farewell peace and prosperity in England. Nothing but temporal misery and ruin will be the consequence! If the *eclipse* brings such misery, what will the full *darkening* of the sun do?

2. The second sin of London is **UNFRUITFULNESS** in such a fertile soil. This sin has been an attendant upon, and a consequent of the former.

London was not only a *Goshen* — but an *Eden*. God chose out London to be his *garden* — he has hedged it, planted, watered, pruned and fertilized it. No place in the world has had more plenty of the means of grace: God has given the former and the latter rain; and sweet dews of Heaven, both morning and evening, did fall upon this place. In the morning seed was sown, and in the evening the hand was not withdrawn. Plentiful and powerful has preaching been in London, in season and out of season, on the Sabbath-day, and on the week-day.

But has London answered all God's care and cost? Has not God come for many years together, seeking fruit, and found nothing but the *leaves of profession?* Has he not often *threatened* to cut down the unfruitful trees, and not allow them to cumber his ground any longer? And when, through the intercession of the vine-dresser, he has spared them this year, and another year — has not the same unfruitfulness still remained? What could the Lord have done more for his vineyard — than what he has done? But when he looked for grapes — it brought forth only leaves or wild grapes? And is it then to be wondered at, if the Lord plucks down the hedge — that it might be eaten by the wild boar and beast of the field; if he break down the wall — and makes it waste and desolate? Is it to be wondered at, if he withholds the clouds that they rain not on it, and allows briars and thorns to spring up in it — where the plants once grew?

The *vine*, when it is unfruitful, is the most unuseful of all trees, Luke 13; Isaiah 5; Ezekiel 15; it is fit for nothing but the fire; and the Lord has threatened to gather the unfruitful branches, and to cast them into the fire and burn them! John 15:6. And the *earth* which drinks in the rain that often falls upon it, and instead of herbs, fit for the use of him by whom it is dressed — brings forth nothing but briars and thorns — God rejects and curses, and in the end burns! Hebrews 6:7.

O the *unfruitfulness* of London! O the *briars* and *thorns* which have flourished in this ground, whereby the seed of the Word has been choked! O the hemlock, the thistle, and the wormwood, that have sprung up in the furrows of the field! O the *tares* that have abounded and overtopped the wheat, and how little good fruit has there been brought forth! O the wild olive-trees which have grown up in God's garden, and wild figs and wild grapes — which the fig-trees and vines of God have yielded unto!

O the *leanness* of his sheep in such fat pasture! O the barrenness! O the barrenness of London, under such plentiful showers of the Word! "Instead of the fruits of righteousness, which are to the praise and glory of God," there have been the fruits of unrighteousness, and wickedness, which are to God's dishonor! Instead of the fruits of the Spirit, which are "love, joy, peace, gentleness, meekness, temperance, goodness, faith;" there have been "the works of the flesh, fornication, immorality, lasciviousness, hatred, variance, anger, strifes, seditions, heresies, envyings, murders, drunkenness, revelings, and such like;" of which the Apostle tells us, "that those who do such things shall not inherit the kingdom of God!"

And those who have not abounded in the grosser works of the

flesh, very few of them have been very *fruitful in good works*. London has had the means of grace — and yet most of them are without grace, and few of them have much grace. London has had powerful ordinances — but what powerful *effect* have they produced? What have they to show of all their prayers, and sermons, and ordinances? Have they attained unto a great measure of mortification? Is grace grown up to a great height?

Give me permission a little more particularly, to instance the unfruitfulness of London in regard of repentance, faith, love, and obedience — the *fruit* which God so much looks for, and so much delights in.

(1.) Where have been the **fruits of repentance** in London?

*Calls* there have been to repentance — frequent, fervent.

*Reason* for repentance — sins numerous, heinous.

*Need* of repentance — that judgments temporal, eternal, might be diverted, that pardon, happiness, might be obtained.

And yet, O the impenitency and hard-heartedness of London! Few bleeding hearts under the sharp sword of the Word; little tenderness under the most melting discourses; few converts and penitent people did the most powerful preaching bring forth in London; converting work was at a great standstill, though there were so many unconverted people in the city! And by the impenitency and hardness of heart in London, God's treasury of wrath has been filled up, which, in some measure, he has opened in these late judgments that he has inflicted! And yet the great day of his wrath is still to come! Romans 2:4, 5.

(2.) Where have been the fruits of **faith** in London? How has unbelief abounded, the great Gospel sin, more dangerous than any other, and more heinous in London than in any other place! O the thick veil of unbelief which has hidden Gospel mysteries, and things afar off from the eyes of this people! O the evil heart of unbelief, which has shut the door against the Lord Jesus Christ, who has knocked so long for entertainment! O the sottishness of London, to believe no more, when *truths* have been so plain and clear; when *promises* have been made known, so great and sure; when *Christ* has been preached and offered; and when Heaven has been revealed and offered! And when all have such need, for the most to shut the eye, and ear, and heart, and through unbelief to refuse; to give God the lie, and turn upon him the back; to give Christ a wound, and tread his blood under foot; to give the Spirit a repulse, and send him away grieved from the heart, as men do by their unbelief — this sin provokes the Lord to great displeasure.

(3.) Where have been the fruits of **love** in London? O the want of love to God, and one to another! The grace of love is necessary and sweet, and has been much pressed — but little *exercised* in London.

There has been much love of the world — but little love of the Father.

Hatred of the brethren has abounded — but there was little brotherly love.

Burning anger there has been — but little burning love.

Burning lusts — but little burning love.

Inordinate carnal love — but little true spiritual love.

Carnal love has exceeded the bounds — but spiritual love has been in a very low degree!

And when love in London has waxed cold, is it a wonder if God's anger has waxed so hot, and broken forth into such flames, as we have seen?

(4.) Where have been the fruits of **obedience** in London — and expression of love to Jesus Christ, by keeping of his commandments, though his commandments are not grievous?

3. A third sin of London, is **hypocrisy in the profession of religion**. This sin exceedingly prevailed in the late times, when profession of religion has grown into *fashion*. Religion was near in the mouths of most — but far from the heart. There was a general face of religion — but it was no more than skin-deep; it was seated in the countenance, not rooted in the heart. How many *painted sepulchers* had we in London, *outwardly* fair and beautiful — but *inwardly* full of rottenness and wickedness. How much *sounding brass* had we then in our streets: a great *noise* and *stir* hypocrites did make — but they were *hollow* at heart! Most of our gold was counterfeit. We had water instead of wine, and dross instead of silver.

O how was religion abused! some made it a *stirrup* to get up by into the seat of honor; others made it a *cloak* to cover their covetous practices; many base and wicked designs were carried on under *pretense of religion.*

It would take too much time to set forth hypocrites in all their shapes, and to paint hypocrisy in all its colors. London has formerly abounded with hypocrites, and more lately it has not been free. If Hell-fire is the portion especially of hypocrites hereafter, Matthew 24:51, no wonder then if God is angry with a place, and punishes it with plague and fire!

4. The fourth sin of London is, **formality** and **lukewarmness** in

the worship of God. There was much formality, when there was no heart; and I suppose that forms have not quickened unto more loveliness; there was a *face of worship* indeed in London; and was there only, or little more, than a face in most places? God is holy and jealous, "a great king, and his name is dreadful," Mal. 1:14.

"God is a Spirit, and those who worship him, must worship him in spirit and in truth," John 4:24. But has his worship been accordingly in London? has there been that spiritual worship which he requires?

Let London seriously reflect upon their behavior towards God in their *devotions*. Have they had a due awe and dread of the great name of God upon them, when they have seemed to draw near unto him? Have they worshiped him with reverence and godly fear? Outward reverence some have used, more than he has required, in bowing at names and before places; but have they had *inward reverence and fear of God upon their hearts?* have they clothed themselves with *humility*, when they have come into his presence? Has there been *inward fervor and delight* accompanying their outward acts of worship?

Alas! how formal has London been, especially of late in God's worship; they have ***prayed*** — but what kind of prayers have they been? Could they deserve the name of prayers? Were those prayers likely to prevent judgment, or turn away wrath?

Some ***confessions*** of sin have been made — but so general and formal, that they have been very unlikely to work up the heart to sorrow and repentance; and where some have been more particular, has not much formality cleaved to them? Where has hearty grief for sin and sorrow been to be found? Would not a small vial hold all the tears that have dropped from the eyes of great assemblies, even in the day of their solemn humiliations? Has not sin been rolled under the tongue, when confession of sin has been at the end of it? Have not the confessions of many been such, as if they came to ask permission to commit sin, rather than humbly to bewail it?

***Petitions*** have been made for pardon, and grace, and sanctification — but has it not been lip-prayer, without hearty desire? Has it not been in such a manner, as if they did not much care whether they did obtain or no? As if they could make shift well enough without a pardon? As if they had no need of grace and holiness — but they must say something for form and custom. Has there not been an enmity in the hearts of many — against that which they have seemed to desire with their lips? who have stirred up themselves to lay hold on God? Who have wrestled in prayer, with fervent desires, with faith, and importunity?

Hearing there has been in London — but how little believing; how little relishing the Word, and receiving it with love! Singing there has been — but how little joy and melody of the heart in the Lord!

O how formal and lukewarm have Londoners been; how much of the Laodicean temper have they had in all ordinances! And might not God say to London, as he did of old to Jerusalem. Isaiah 1:11-14, "To what purpose is the multitude of your sacrifices unto me?" etc. Such services are to no purpose; they are vain worship, and do not attain the end thereof, either to profit him that offers them — or to please him unto whom they are offered.

Can such *formal services* be effectual to procure pardon or peace? Can they bear up the spirit in a day of trouble? Will not the morning cloud and early dew of such *righteousness* flee away and vanish upon the approach of the sun? Will not such spiders' webs be broken to pieces by a stormy wind? How do formalists behave themselves, as if they had no religion — when they fall into troubles! When God thunders by his judgments — what can a cold, formal, empty prayer do? When Death appears before them with a grim countenance — what comfort can such reap by reflection on such formal services? What evidences for Heaven can they gather from any of their external devotions?

And are not they to as little purpose in regard of God? May not God say unto them of their fastings and prayers, "Did you fast unto me? Did you pray at all unto me?" Zech. 7:5. Or, as here to the Jews, that he was sick of their services, even to a loathing; that he took no delight in them; and "The multitude of your sacrifices — what are they to me? I have more than enough of burnt offerings, of rams and the fat of fattened animals; I have no pleasure in the blood of bulls and lambs and goats. When you come to appear before me, who has asked this of you, this trampling of my courts? Stop bringing meaningless offerings! Your incense is detestable to me. New Moons, Sabbaths and convocations — I cannot bear your evil assemblies. Your New Moon festivals and your appointed feasts, my soul hates. They have become a burden to me; I am weary of bearing them. When you spread out your hands in prayer, I will hide my eyes from you; even if you offer many prayers, I will not listen!" Isaiah 1:11-15

"I hate, I despise your religious feasts; I cannot stand your assemblies. Even though you bring me burnt offerings and grain offerings, I will not accept them. Though you bring choice fellowship offerings, I will have no regard for them. Away with the noise of your songs! I will not listen to the music of your harps!"

The Lord is much offended with formal, hypocritical services; hereby they flatter and mock him — and is he deceived with flatteries? Such services are like a dead, cold, black, mangled, rotten, stinking carcass, without the soul and spirit, which must needs be very unsavory and displeasing. They are like the lame, blind, halt, sick cattle, which were not fit to be offered up in sacrifice under the law, Mal. 1:8. "When you bring blind animals for sacrifice, is that not wrong? When you sacrifice crippled or diseased animals, is that not wrong? Try offering them to your governor! Would he be pleased with you? Would he accept you? says the Lord Almighty!" And will God then be pleased?

Such people, while they seem to serve God with their outward man — they really serve the devil and their own lusts, with their inward man.

God has the form — the devil has the heart;
God has the show — the devil has the substance;
God has the bark, the rind, the shell — the devil has the kernel;
God has the cabinet — the devil gets the jewel;

they give God the devil's leavings, and refuse, as it were, of their own lusts; for they spend the strength and vigor of soul and body, in serving the devil, and gratifying their own lusts — and then think to put God off with anything; giving him only some dead, cold, faint, empty, heartless, lifeless, outward services. And even in them, they are swayed by some carnal motives, which are the secret spring to the wheel of all external services. And O how abominable is all such formal worship in the sight of God! "These people honor Me with their lips, but their heart is far from Me. They worship Me in vain!" Matthew 15:8-9

Has not formality in worship been one sin of London which has helped to fill up the Ephah? When the means God has appointed for the turning away of his anger, is used in such a manner, that itself becomes a *provocation* — then it is no wonder if his wrath breaks forth without remedy!

5. A fifth sin of London, is **division** among professors. Different persuasions have made wide breaches and divisions in London, and through divisions, have arisen great animosities and contentions, unto the shame of Christianity and the Protestant religion; and has not God been provoked to anger hereby? Has not he contended with professors, and by the common scourge he has

brought upon them, called aloud unto them for a union, and more hearty accord and affection than formerly they have had? And has not he given them liberty and opportunity, had they minded and cared to make use of it, for meeting together in order unto healing? But have professors of different parties been sensible of God's meaning in the scourge upon their backs? Have they hearkened unto God's call? Have they laid hold of and improved opportunities for closing up their wide breaches? I hope there has been some increase in affection among some; but how rarely has it been to be found; and when there are such breaches still among us, is it not just with God to make further breaches upon us, as he has done by his judgments.

6. A sixth sin of London, is **neglect of reformation**. Neglect of:

1. Personal reformation,
2. Family reformation,
3. City reformation,
4. Church reformation.

(1.) Neglect of **PERSONAL reformation** in heart and life. Who in London have seriously and very diligently endeavored the reformation of their **HEARTS**? When so unclean and polluted — who has labored to get them washed? When such roots of bitterness have been springing forth, and such weeds of lust have been growing there — who has endeavored to pluck them up? Outward neatness there has been in London, washing and rinsing, rubbing and scouring — but O, the *inward sluttishness!* Those who have had clean houses and clean garments, and clean faces and hands — have had foul hearts!

Who has taken care every day to rinse and scour their inside? to bring their hearts to the fountain set open for sin and immorality; and to cleanse themselves from all filthiness of flesh and spirit, that they might arrive every day unto greater perfection in holiness? Those who have been careful to dress their *bodies* every day — have been very careless in dressing their *hearts*, neglecting to put on the white robes of Christ's righteousness, which alone can cover their spiritual nakedness and deformity; and to get the jewels of grace, which alone can adorn the soul, and render it amiable in the sight of God.

"Above all else, guard your heart, for it is the wellspring of life!" Proverbs 4:23. Heart-work is **hard**-work; and it is so hard, that most have let it alone; they have been discouraged with the difficulty; the opposition of Satan and lust to this work, has been so strong, that they have been quickly overpowered, upon their first attempts and endeavors after a change and rectifying of the disorders which they have perceived.

Heart-work is **secret**-work. Many have employed themselves in the more open work of religion — few have taken pains with their hearts in secret. Many take heed . . .

to their *tongues* — what they speak;
to their *hands* — what they do;
to their *feet* — where they go;

but few take heed to their *hearts!* Murder, adultery, theft, and the like sins have been committed in the heart by many, who would have been afraid and ashamed of the outward acts.

O the unwatchfulness there has been in London over the heart! Citizens have watched their *gates*, and watched their *streets*, and watched their *houses*. But how few have watched their *hearts*, what comes in, and what goes forth! How few have set a watch before the door of their lips, and ears, and other senses — which are the inlets of sin; and upon their hearts, from whence are the outlets of sin! How few have kept their hearts with all diligence; how few have labored to govern their thoughts, to rule their passions, to subjugate their wills to Christ; and to deliver up all their affections to his disposal and obedience! Heart-reformation has been much neglected.

Who in London have endeavored **LIFE**-reformation as they should? How few have there been effectually persuaded to put away the evil of their doings, from before the eyes of the Lord, to cease from evil, and learn to do well. How few have broken off their sins by repentance, and thoroughly amended their ways, measuring out their actions by the rule of the Word! How few have got the law of God written in their *hearts*, and the transcript thereof in their *lives*, exemplifying the precepts thereof in their conversations! How few in London have been like so many *Epistles of Christ*, in whom the will and grace of their Master might be read! Who have trodden in Christ's steps, walking as he walked, and followed him in the way of obedience and self-denial? Who have shined like so many lights in dark places and times, adorning their profession, and living as befits the Gospel?

Great *irregularities* there have been in the lives of most Londoners:

little Gospel-reformation;
little making religion the main business of life;
little holy exact living.

If a stranger had looked into our city, and observed the lives of the most, and not known them to have had the *name* of Christians — would not we have judged them to be heathens, yes many of them in their dealing to be worse than Turks and Infidels? Thus personal reformation has been neglected.

(2.) A great neglect there has been of **FAMILY reformation** in London. How few have, with Joshua, *resolved*, and accordingly *endeavored* — that they and their houses should serve the Lord! How few have set up religious worship in their families! Have not many hundred houses in the city been without family prayer in them from one end of the week to the other? And is it strange, that the Lord has burned down those houses wherein the inhabitants would not vouchsafe to worship him?

And where there has been *some* prayer in many families, it was but once a day, and that so late at night, and when the body has been so tired and sleepy, and the soul so dull and unfit for God's service — that the prayers have been no prayers, or lost prayers — such which, instead of pleasing him, have provoked him to anger? How few labor to instruct their families, catechize their children; to bring them up in the nurture and admonition of the Lord. Has not God threatened to pour out his wrath upon irreligious families? Jeremiah 10:25.

(3.) Neglect of **CITY reformation**. Have not the magistrates of London been faulty here? Let them ask their own consciences, whether to the uttermost of their power, according to the trust and opportunity the Lord has put into their hands, they have endeavored the reformation of the city? Whether, as God's under-officers, they have improved their interest for the promotion of religion in the zealous exercise of it? yes, whether they have put the laws made, into execution against swearers and drunkards — endeavoring to find out and punish such offenders?

(1.) Neglect of **CHURCH reformation**. And is there no blame to be laid upon church officers? Has there been that zeal for, and faithful execution of *church discipline*, according to the rules of the Word? Has not the Lord Jesus Christ been affronted in his kingly office, by some who have imposed precepts of their own, upon men's consciences, instead of vigorously endeavoring the execution of his; and taken the power of the keys out of the hands of those unto whom the Lord has entrusted it, hereby rendering the execution of discipline impossible, according to the laws of Christ? Have not the tender and most conscientious lain under the censures of some, rather than the openly profane, and scandalously wicked?

Neglect of reformation am I speaking of? Nay, have not many who call themselves *ministers*, endeavored rather the overthrow than the promotion of it? Have they not had sneers in the pulpits at holiness and zealous profession, which they have seconded by a conversation of dissoluteness, malicious opposition, and persecution of those especially, who have been the most pious? Sad neglects there have been of reformation in London, and that when London lay under such obligations to reform; as Christians, they were obliged, by baptismal and renewed vows; as Protestants of the Reformed religion, they were obliged to endeavor a reformation; by mercies they were obliged; and have they been under no other obligations? And has not the neglect of reformation, notwithstanding all obligations, rendered them guilty of deceit, infidelity, yes, of perjury itself? I truly believe this is the great sin God is scourging London for; God is contending for a reformation, and if they do not endeavor it more vigorously, the sooner, I fear, he will bring desolation upon them.

7. A seventh sin of London, is fearful **apostasy**, and a spirit of **compliance with the sins of the times**. How many in London, who formerly were *great professors*, have revealed themselves to be rotten hypocrites; who, casting off the sheep's clothing, and laying aside all profession, have given themselves up to dissoluteness and licentious living. Formerly they have *seemed* true penitents, and to "be washed from their iniquities;" but they "have returned with the dog to the vomit, and with the sow that is washed, to the wallowing in the mire!" Formerly they have been swept a little within, and garnished outwardly with a fair profession; "but the unclean spirit has returned," and without any great difficulty "has entered with seven worse spirits, and defiled them more than before, and made their last state worse than their first!" Matthew 12:43-45. I speak not so much of those who worship God in this mode, or that mode, and of alterations herein; but of those who sometimes professed religion, and now do not worship God in any mode at all; but wholly addict themselves to their lusts, and are ashamed to be called or thought to be pious.

They would not now *look* like a saint, or *speak* like a saint, much less *live* like a saint. Thus have many, in our days, cast off all fear of God, and devoted themselves, with the Hell-hounds of the times, to the service of the devil, resolving to do what in them lies, to promote the interest of his kingdom. And if some are a little more awkward in his service, and not altogether so like him, and such apt scholars presently, as others whose education has been in his school from their childhood — yet they learn very fast, and their proficiency in a short time is astonishing. And in regard of apostasy, they come nearer the *image of the devil* than those that have been always tutored by him.

Now, for any in London to forsake God — that they might serve the devil; to draw off from the ways of holiness — that they might walk in the ways of wickedness — casts a great slur upon God and his ways! They do, in effect, say, that the devil is a better master than God; and that the way of sin, which leads to Hell — is more desirable than the way of holiness, which alone can bring to Heaven. The Lord threatens, "that his soul shall have no pleasure in such" apostates, Hebrews 10:38.

See how God pleads with apostatizing Israel, "Has a nation ever changed its gods? (Yet they are not gods at all.) But my people have exchanged their Glory for worthless idols. Be appalled at this, O heavens, and shudder with great horror, declares the Lord. My people have committed two sins: They have forsaken me, the spring of living water, and have dug their own cisterns, broken cisterns that cannot hold water!" Jeremiah 2:11-13

And hence follows, verse 15, "Lions have roared; they have growled at him. They have laid waste his land; his towns are burned and deserted!" And verse 17, "Have you not brought this on yourselves by forsaking the Lord your God when he led you in the way?" and verse 19, "Your wickedness will punish you; your backsliding will rebuke you. Consider then and realize how evil and bitter it is for you when you forsake the Lord your God and have no awe of me, declares the Lord, the Lord Almighty!" And may not God thus plead with the apostates of London, and punish them as he did his people of Israel?

8. The eighth sin of London is **deafening the ear against all God's calls**.

The Lord has called upon London by his *ministers* — but they have been like the deaf adder, which will not hearken to the voice of the charmer; they have stopped the ears, and turned away their shoulder, and made their heart like an adamant stone!

God has called by his *mercies* — but this voice has been too low, and they have slept the more securely in sin.

God, after other means, has called — by afflictions, first lighter, then heavier; and yet how many in London have, and still do walk contrary unto God, and will not return to him who has smitten them. They have been *incorrigible* under all God's *correcting rods!*

When God spoke by the *plague*, they were a little awakened — but quickly dropped asleep again! When the plague was a little over, they return to their trades again, to their *sins* again — but they do not return unto the *Lord.* And when the judgment of the plague was so much lost, and ineffectual for their good, this, no doubt, has provoked God so quickly and unexpectedly to turn his hand upon them, and bring the judgment of the fire! And if they will still walk contrary to God, they must expect that God will walk contrary to them, until he has *consumed* them!

9. A ninth sin of London is **profaneness**, and a loose and frothy spirit, especially in the youth and upspringing generation. I do not tax all; for I am confident there is a serious and a godly youth growing up. But O that there were not reason to say, that the generality of youth is profane and wicked, as well as those who are grown more mature in wickedness! And this profaneness has showed itself in:

1. Profane using God's *name*;
2. Profane breaking of God's *day*;
3. Profane scoffing at God's *people.*

1. In profane using of **God's NAME**. How grossly has the third commandment been broken in the city. How has the great and dreadful name of the Lord God, which should make men to tremble in the mention of it, and command their spirits into awe and reverence — been vainly taken by many, and used to fill up the sentence of their ordinary discourse. And not only so — but how has the name of God been tossed in the *black mouths* of the children of darkness, and even torn in pieces by their hideous oaths and execrations. What a Hellish noise has the sound of full-mouthed oaths, made sometimes in the streets, enough to make the hair stand on end, of one who has a sense of the greatness of that majesty upon his heart, which hereby is so audaciously affronted.

Oh the swearing that has been used by Londoners in buying and selling! Many *parents* have been so addicted to this sin in their families, that their little children have no sooner learned to speak — but they have also learned of them to *swear* by the name of God, which has been all the teaching of God that they have given them — a devilish teaching indeed, which hereafter they will curse them for in Hell!

But if you should have laid your ears unto the taverns, and alehouses, and whore-houses, and other devil-houses, once standing in London — and hearkened to the speeches of many of the devil's imps, in their drinking and gaming, and other lewd practices, especially when a little crossed and vexed — O what *language of Hell* might have been heard! How have those cursed villains, in the heat of their wine and anger, shot volleys of oaths in the face of the God of Heaven! and whetting their tongues like a sharp sword, they have not feared to wound the name of God, when they have received any injury from men. O what *poison of asps* has there been under their lips! But a worse poison of *sin* in their hearts, from the evil treasure and abundance of which, these oaths and blasphemies have proceeded.

But who can find words to set forth the *evil* of this sin, which has not the temptation of pleasure, advantage, or honor, as other sins have — and therefore is a great proof of a monstrously wicked heart? And who can express God's displeasure for this sin, for which he makes sometimes a whole land to mourn? And has not this sin provoked the Lord to utter his angry voice in *plaguing* and *burning* of the city, that they might fear to abuse his name any more?

(2.) In profane breaking of **God's DAY**. Sabbath-breaking was an ordinary sin in London. I say not, it was so much broken in doing the ordinary works of the particular callings — but in that which was worse: how many did spend the Sabbath in eating to excess and drinking until they were drunk, in sleeping, in sports and recreations. Many wholly neglected the worship of God on that day; and instead of that — did the devil more service on the Lord's day, than all the days of the week besides!

The many weeks of Sabbaths which London had in the time of the plague, methinks did reprove London for their profaning of the weekly Sabbath. And the great fire, (I will not call it bon-fire, because so destructive to London) which was begun in the city on the Lord's day, did reprove London for those lesser fires, (I will not call them bon-fires, because so offensive to God) which not long before were kindled in the streets on that day, which called for other kind of work. Not to speak anything, whether there were any just occasion for those fires and ringing of bells, (most of which were melted before they were rung so generally again) and such a show of mirth and rejoicing at that time.

The citizens carrying forth their goods, and lying in the fields with grief and fear, might put them in mind how often they had walked out into those fields on the Lord's day for their recreation: when they should rather have been hearing the Word preached, or if that were over, repeating it in their own families, giving and receiving instruction, or in their closets at the throne of grace, or employed in meditation. As God delights in those that call "his Sabbaths a delight," and makes sweet promises to them; so he is highly *displeased* with Sabbath-breakers, and has denounced severe threatenings against them, Jeremiah 17:27, "If you will not hearken to me to hallow the Sabbath-day; I will kindle a fire in the gates of Jerusalem which shall devour the palaces thereof, and shall not be quenched!"

3. In profane scoffing at **God's PEOPLE**. The name of a saint, and godly man, has been ridiculous to many profane spirits in London, and used by them in a way of reproach. How have God's people, especially the more strict and zealous, been made the drunkard's song, and laughed at in the streets. Horrid impiety! As if it were matter of more shame to be like the holy God — than to be like the foul devil! and to be employed in the work of angels — than to drudge in Satan's chains!

No wonder if God is angry with such a place, where such *vipers* have had their abode! Profaneness is a great sin that has brought ruin upon us.

10. A tenth sin of London is **PRIDE**. This sin being . . .

so odious to God;
so destructive where it abounds;

and so universal in London —

I shall speak of it the more largely, both in regard of the inward workings, and the outward expressions of it: which, when opened, I believe there are none that will be able to say they are wholly free from it.

(1.) In regard of the **inward workings of pride**. Oh how has the poison of this sin envenomed the spirits of the most in a very high degree. How many *self-admirers* have there been in London, who have been puffed up with an overweening conceit of their own excellencies; what high, towering, swelling thoughts have they had of themselves! What secret self-pleasing, and lifting up themselves in their own esteem. Some esteeming themselves for that which is matter of shame! Some admiring themselves for their own wit and abilities, when they have lain fallow, and not been employed for God, or when they have been employed to his dishonor. Some admiring themselves when they have been wise — but it has been to do evil. Some admiring themselves when they have been men of understanding — but it has been to practice iniquity. Some admiring themselves when they have had cunning craftiness —

but it has been to deceive, to defraud, and over-reach, or to plot and contrive others' mischief! Some admiring themselves when they have had a sharp wit, quick understanding, rich imagination, fluency of speech: but the employment has been about toys and trifles, or that which is worse, when the vent has been in jesting with Scripture, scoffing at the pious, or in dirty and obscene discourses!

Others have admired themselves, for that which really they never had — but only in their own imagination. Some for their abilities and learning; thinking themselves great scholars when none have thought so but themselves. Others have admired themselves for their grace and godliness, when their silver has been dross; and their grace either counterfeit in whole, or so mixed with unperceived corruption, that upon examination they would find themselves very poor, in that which they thought themselves so much enriched with; and if they looked to the root and principle of their actions, they might find great flaws, and deficiency in those things which they had the highest conceit of!

How many in London have had very honorable esteem of themselves — preferring themselves above others, yes, above the whole world. Few have measured themselves by the Scripture rule — but measured themselves by their own imaginations, or by other men's esteem. How many have thought themselves to be something — when they have been nothing; and rejoiced in their actions as excellent and admirable, not from their own proof and trial of them by the Word; but from others' acceptance and commendations, and by comparing them with the actions of others, whom they have imagined themselves to exceed.

O how have some lifted up themselves above others, looking upon themselves as far more worthy — yet without any real ground. Their eye has been upon their own good things, overlooking the secret evil, because it cannot be seen by men. And their eye has been upon others' flaws, overlooking the good which has been out of ready view. *Their eye has been upon their own best things — and upon others' worst things; aggravating their faults — and extenuating their own.* Thus they have in their thoughts brought others down through uncharitableness, and lifted up themselves upon the ruins, which their uncharitableness has made in others' worth! And when they have had greater esteem because of their greater *show* — this high opinion of themselves has been confirmed. Whereas, in truth, others who made less show, and had less esteem, have had more sincerity, and secret hidden excellency.

I might further trace the inward workings of pride in the *self-love* which it has effected; what a astonishing affection have proud people had towards themselves, notwithstanding their ugliness and spiritual deformity, the rottenness and corruption within them, and many lusts of their hearts; all which pride has covered! They have a thousand faults in themselves — and *pride* has put a fair gloss and varnish upon them all — and has represented men to themselves, as very lovely and amiable.

Pride also has chosen for such, their friends, who have been loved, not according to the worth which those people have had; but according to the estimation those people have had of their worth, which, if those have fallen in estimation, these have fallen in affection.

I might show the workings of pride, in the hatred, anger, spite, revenge, which it has effected, when it has met with disesteem or slighting. I might show the workings of pride, in the solicitous thoughts and cares concerning, and eager prodding and pursuit after others' commendations; and the storm of commotion and disturbance which this wind has raised, when the *tide of applause* has run another way. I might show the workings of pride, in the complacency and delight it has yielded in drinking out of a full stream of others' esteem, in chewing the cud, and revolving in the mind the praise of men. But so much concerning the *inward* workings of pride.

(2.) Concerning the **outward expressions of pride**:

1. Pride in **SPEECH**. London has been grossly guilty in *boasting* and *vain-glory*. You could come into almost any company — and you would find many boasting people! Some foaming out the shame of their own praise in high expressions, and direct self-commendations, (without any regard to God's glory) but they have done it only to be well thought on, and admired! Others are driveling out their own praises more *slyly* and *indirectly*. But a Christian of eyes and brains, might easily perceive that the drift and scope of the discourse has been *self*, and a tacit begging of a good opinion. As if one should say, "Dear friends, think a little better of me; have me higher in your esteem, for to say the truth, by this I give you to understand that I am a very worthy person."

Many we shall find very forward to "declare their own goodness" — but few faithful in speaking forth the praises of God; yes, many there have been, who have *discommended* themselves, not that they might fall — but rise in esteem of others. Thus some rotten-hearted hypocrites, as full of pride as they can hold, and some sincere in the main — yet too much like them — have spoken so lowly of themselves, and so much against themselves, as none other would do; and what has been the design? Even that they might be *accounted humble*! And therefore they have taken care in their self-commendations, to speak of nothing but *common infirmities*, concealing their more gross faults; and those common infirmities, in a mourning and complaining way, as if they were very sensible of them, as if affected, afflicted, and burdened with them (as the humble, sincere Christian is indeed) — but only that they might be esteemed for sensibility of small faults. And then they have taken care to commend themselves, not to those that are more quick-sighted Christians — for they would quickly have smelt out their pride; but unto those, who they have looked upon as the most tender, charitable people, who are ready hereby to advance them higher in esteem; or to weaker Christians, who are ready to confess more evil of themselves.

And when they have thus *spoken* against themselves, they have not really *thought* so — but the contrary; but they have spoken so, that they might be contradicted, and commended to their faces! If they thought they should have fallen in esteem by such words — they would have held their peace; but because they supposed *discommendation* might most effectually promote them, and draw out a good word, therefore they have used it.

Proud hypocrites speak poorly of themselves — that they may be *accounted* humble! But they cannot endure to *be* humble. They care nothing for grace, yes, they hate it; yet they would be thought to have it, because it does promote esteem! They love the *reward* of humility — but they care not for humility *itself*. They love humility in others — because such people will stoop to them; but they love not humility in themselves — for they will stoop to none.

Thus some also, out of a secret design of pride, have slandered others behind their backs, that they might be thought to exceed them, whom they find fault with! They have labored to bring down others — that they might set up themselves. And the same design of pride they have had in commending others to their faces, and exalting them in words above their desert — not from a real esteem which they have had of them — but only that they might draw forth a commendation from them; such expressions of pride have been to be found in many professors.

2. Pride in **CLOTHES** has been more gross, and open, and general in the city. We read of the pride of the daughters of Jerusalem,

Isaiah 3:16, etc. "the daughters of Zion are haughty, walking with heads held high and seductive eyes, going along with prancing steps, jingling their ankle bracelets!" And what it was they were proud of, see from verse 18 to 25, "The bangles and headbands and crescent necklaces, the earrings and bracelets and veils, the headdresses and ankle chains and sashes, the perfume bottles and charms, the signet rings and nose rings, the fine robes and the capes and cloaks, the purses and mirrors, and the linen garments and tiaras and shawls," and the like. And has there not been this pride in London? Were not the daughters of London like the daughters of Zion — for pride and haughtiness? Was there any place in England that could show such *pride of apparel* as London could show, which not only the female gender were guilty of? Were there any fashions, though ever so foolish and apish, which London did not presently imitate? Who can count the cost which has been lavished out in clothing and rich apparel; some pinching their bellies and families — to lay it out on this lust.

This pride of *apparel* is very shameful and absurd, clothes being the *badge of apostasy*, which were not made use of until after the fall. It is as if a thief should be proud of his shackles, or any malefactor of his mark of disgrace! At least the gaudy attire of many people has signified the *emptiness* and *frothy mind within*; and that they have had nothing to set them forth — but their clothes!

I might also add, the pride, which the daughters of London have had of their **BEAUTY**, though it be but skin-deep. *The body is but a skin full of dirt;* and the choicest beauty without wisdom, is like a jewel hung on the ear or nose of a swine! The Lord knows what monstrous, and defiled, and deformed *insides* — the most of those have had, who have been so fair and adorned *outwardly*.

Many in London have been proud of their fine clothes, and fair faces; and others of their fair shops, and stately houses! *Pride* has hung about the neck like a chain, and covered them like a garment — instead of the clothing and ornament of humility, which before God is of so great price.

Now God is highly offended with the *sin of pride*, "God resists the proud," 1 Peter 5:5. He does, as it were, set himself in battle array against them. "Pride goes before destruction, and a haughty spirit before a fall," Proverbs 16:18. Pride was one of Sodom's sins — which city was burnt with fire from Heaven, Ezekiel 16:49. The Scriptures speak of three cities that were burnt for this *sin of pride* among other sins — namely, Sodom, Jerusalem, and Babylon. And may not London come in for a fourth? The blotches and ulcers, and loathsome sores in the bodies of many, when the *plague* was in London; and the burning of so much *fuel of pride*, by the *fire* — methinks were a very loud reproof and rebuke of London for this sin.

11. An eleventh sin of London, is *fullness of bread*, or **intemperance in eating**. This was another of the sins of Sodom. God had fed London with the finest of the wheat, and gave plenty of grain, and meat, and other provisions; but how have they abused plenty by their *intemperance* and *luxury*. O the excessive feasting in halls, and private houses, of those whose estates have been more plentiful! What indulging has there been to the appetite, as if *self-denial* in regard of the *appetite* were no duty — or an *enemy*, and with the poor to be shut out of doors! What delicacy and daintiness of *palate*, have many in London had — so that air, earth, sea, must be ransacked to please them, and all would not do! What loathing have they had of ordinary food! Many good creatures of God must be cut, and mangled, and spoiled — to make them new dishes; which, however pleasing, have but spoiled their stomachs, and bred diseases in their bodies. Some have not eaten much — but they have been so *choice*, that scarcely any food has pleased them; and that not through sickness of body — but wantonness of mind!

Others have been pleased with their food, and over-pleased, and all their pleasure has been therein — all "whose god," as the apostle speaks, Philippians 3:19, "has been their belly." Such, like the rich man, Luke 16:19, "have fared sumptuously and deliciously every day." O the excessive *cost* that some have bestowed upon their tables daily! O the excessive *quantity* of food that some have devoured! O the excessive *time* that has been wasted in *pampering the flesh!* What *rioting* and *banqueting* has there been daily in London, many feeding themselves without fear, as if *gluttony* were not any sin at all. How many have been like fed horses in the city, or like fattened oxen, who, as the Apostle James speaks, "have lived in pleasure, and been wanton, and fattened themselves as in a day of slaughter," James 5:5. And as Hosea 13:6. "When I fed them, they were satisfied; when they were satisfied, they became proud; then they forgot me!"

This kind of *intemperance* has so strangely *brutified* many, that they have been even degenerated into beasts, only that they have been more unuseful; for hereby they have unfitted themselves for all kind of service, as if they were *born only to eat!* But they have only prepared themselves for those *ruining and slaughtering judgments* which have come upon the city.

12. A twelfth sin of London is **IDLENESS**. This is a consequence of the former; only that idleness has been more widespread. This was also a sin of Sodom; I will not say, but many citizens of London were diligent in their calling — but how many idle vagrant people were there in the city?

Though eating, and drinking, and clothing were *necessary*, and called for *some* time; yet the *excess of time spent about these things*, if not worse things — was no better than idle time! Many, especially of the females in the city, have spent so much time in the morning in their beds, if not in sleeping, at least in idle foolish imaginations. They often spend so much time afterwards, in pretty and fancy dressing their bodies — that they have had no time before dinner for prayer or reading, no time to dress their *souls*. And the afternoon being far spent in eating and drinking, and the rest of the time has run away either in visitings or entertainments, wherein, (if not worse) vain, idle, unprofitable things have been the chief, if not the only subject of their discourse! And by that time they have again refreshed them with food in the evening — they have been too sleepy and unfit for prayer, and the service of God. And thus many careless women in the city have lived in ease and idleness from one end of the week, and one end of the year, unto another.

But methinks the Lord has, by his terrible things in London, spoken unto them much in the same language as he did, "Listen, you women who *lie around in ease*. Listen to me, you who are so smug. In a short time — just a little more than a year — you careless ones will suddenly begin to care. For your fruit crops will fail, and the harvest will never take place. Tremble, you *women of ease*; throw off your complacency. Strip off your pretty clothes, and put on sackcloth to show your grief!" Isaiah 32:9-11

But I would not charge this sin of idleness only upon the female gender: many men have been more shamefully guilty, especially those who have mis-spent so much time in gaming, (not to speak of dressing, eating and drinking, and other time-consuming sins, which are reproved in their proper place.) O the time that many have spent in gaming! Some recreations, wherein the body is *exercised*, may be lawful and necessary at some times — so they do not steal away too much of their time and affections. But for men to sit at *games* as hard as scholars at their books — what rational plea can be used for such wicked idleness?

Thus silver and gold, and great estates have been consumed! And O the golden hours, the days and nights, and precious time, that have been lost in gaming! Thus some have become bankrupt, and moved into the country to hide their shame, after their high place in the city. Some have gone into the high-ways, not to beg — but to do that which is far worse, which in some has had a dreadful conclusion (suicide). And not only this kind of idleness has brought poverty — but also that heedless, slothful spirit, which many of the city have had in their callings; which has made them blemishes to the city, and has been an helper on of our ruin!

13. A thirteenth sin of London is **UNMERCIFULNESS**, another of Sodom's sins, (Ezekiel 16:49). "Now this was the sin of your sister *Sodom*: She and her daughters were arrogant, overfed and unconcerned; *they did not help the poor and needy.*" I shall not blame the whole population for this sin, for the charity of London has sounded throughout the land, and throughout the world. But yet, have not many of the great men of the city been guilty of unmercifulness, who, though more able — yet have been less forward to contribute to the relief of such as have been in distress?

It has been the comfort of some who have lost much by the fire — that they had saved what before they had given to the poor — by putting it out of the reach of moth, or rust, or thieves, or flames of fire. But O, what *marble-hearts* have some had towards the poor! So that whatever *abundance* they had beyond what they themselves did need — they would as soon give so many drops of their blood, as pieces of money, though to help some of the needy and distressed members of Jesus Christ! Not considering that the Lord Jesus is the heir of all things, and whatever estate they had, they were but *his stewards*; and that relief of the needy is a *debt*, which, though *man* cannot require it of them — yet *God* can. And it is unequal, if for lack of payment of God's debts (which they owed out of their estates, by virtue of God's command, to the poor) if the Lord has dispossessed them of his houses, and burned them with fire, and taken away part of the estates which he gave them — because they have employed them no more for his glory.

14. A fourteenth sin of London is **IMMORALITY** — another sin of Sodom; their sin indeed was *unnatural* immorality. I would hope that this sin of *homosexuality* has been little known and practiced in London. But *fornication* and *adultery* have been all too common. Indeed, there has not been that boldness and impudence in this sin as elsewhere; there has not been that *whore's-forehead* (Jeremiah 3:3) so generally in London, declaring their iniquity like Sodom. But let the *consciences* of many Londoners speak — whether they have not been secretly guilty of this sin? Would it not be a

shame to tell of the sleeping around, and wantonness, and secret lewdness which has been committed in London?

Suppose that in all the remaining churches, the sin of immorality should be reproved; and all, both men and women, who have been actually guilty of it — should be forced by an inward sting of conscience, immediately to leave the church. What a *stir* would there be in some churches; what an *emptying* of some pews; what a clearing of some aisles; and how few would there be remaining in some places!

Suppose God put a *visible mark* upon the foreheads of all the adulterers and fornicators in the city of London — as He put a mark upon *Cain* after he had been guilty of murder. Would not many, who walk now very uprightly, and with much seeming innocency — walk with blushes in their cheeks? Would not many keep to their houses and hide their face, and not stir abroad, except in the *night?* Or if in the *day*, would they not shuffle through the streets, and hate the fashion of *little hats*, and the mode of wearing them on top their head? Would they not rather get such hats, whose *brims* are of a larger size; which would the more conveniently cover their brows? And would not many unsuspected and seemingly modest *women* also, stain their cheeks with a vermilion dye upon their husbands' or friends' search into their face? Would not many of them walk with long hoods to cover their foreheads — that they might hide their shame from the view of man?

This sin is so nasty and filthy, that whatever swinish pleasure is found in the commission of it, usually those who are guilty (unless their forehead is made of brass) are ashamed that it should be known! Yet the holy and jealous eye of God has seen them in their filthiness! Their secret sins are set in the light of His countenance, which above all should make them ashamed and afraid! "God will judge the adulterer and all the sexually immoral!" Hebrews 13:4

I have heard of Smithfield haunts, and Moorfield walks, where there has been too great a resort from the city under the shadow of the wings of the night, about these deeds of darkness. The many *whore-houses*, under the name of *ale-houses*, around London, by report, have had too many customers.

Have not some made *their own houses* little better, some men bringing in their whores in little better than public view. And some of the women, by their half-naked breasts, and their immodest attire and demeanor, have enticed the lewd eye; and after basely prostituted their bodies to the lusts of filthy ruffians. O the *boiling, burning lusts* that have been in London! O the wanton eyes and looks! O the *mental* immorality, and secret self-pollutions! O the obscene and filthy speeches! O the toying and lustful dalliances! O the gross actual immorality — which God has been witness to every day in London!

This sin of immorality . . .

debases the *spirit*, made at first after God's own image;
defiles both *soul* and *body*, which
should be the temple of the Holy Spirit;

and renders men unfit for communion with a holy God, who is of such pure eyes that he cannot approve of the least iniquity, much less of this, which is so gross; and not only so — but exceedingly provokes him unto anger and jealousy.

This may be one sin that has brought down such fearful judgments upon the city! We read of twenty-four thousand who died in one day by the plague — for the sin of fornication, Numbers 15:9. And have not many thousand inhabitants and habitations of London, fallen for this sin? It is said of the Israelites, Hosea 7:6. "Their hearts are like an oven. Their passion smolders all night; in the morning it blazes like a flaming fire." Have not the hearts of many in London been like an oven for lust, and themselves putting fuel into it, and stirring it up! And if while they have lain in wait, and have not had present opportunity for satisfaction of their lusts, they have seemed to be asleep — no sooner has the morning light, than a fit occasion offered itself to their adulterous eyes — but their adulterous hearts have burned within them, and has broken forth into a flaming fire, in the actual commission of the horrid sin!

And has not the cursed leaven of *this common sin of the times* spread itself also in London? Therefore the Lord also has made ready his wrath as in an hot oven; and though he has seemed to sleep while he lays in wait, and delayed to execute his judgments; yet in the morning of his great provocation, by this and other sins — his anger has broke forth like a flaming fire, from whence that fire has been kindled which has burnt the greatest part of London down to the ground! "They are well-fed, lusty stallions, each neighing for another man's wife. Should I not punish them for this? declares the Lord. Should I not avenge myself on such a nation as this?" Jeremiah 5:8-9

15. A fifteenth sin of London is **DRUNKENNESS**. This sin has been more visible and apparent. I believe that scarcely any nation under Heaven has proportionably more *taverns* and *ale-houses* than England, and no place in England so many as London, and

its adjacent parts! Besides, there are many *private houses* where this sin has been practiced. How have men "risen early in the morning, to follow strong drink, and continued unto night, until wine inflamed them!" Isaiah 5:11. "Come, they say , and I will fetch wine, and we will fill ourselves with strong drink, and tomorrow shall be as this day, and much more abundant!" Isaiah 56:12.

The rooms and beds full of vomit,
the reelings about the streets,
the contentions and wranglings,
"the wounds without cause, the redness of the eyes,"
and such like, have been too evident a demonstration of men's "tarrying too long at the wine," and distempering themselves with excessive drinking, Proverbs 23:29, 30.

To be overtaken with drunkenness is a great sin, which makes men more *brutish* than their very horses — who will not exceed their measure in drinking!

Soberness prevents many distempers of body, and worse distempers of mind; and, which is worst of all, much dishonor of God, as well as of themselves, which excess in this kind has been the cause of. But for men to follow after this sin, and make it their trade and common practice, to delight in it, and seek for their god and chief happiness in a cup of wine or ale, and to boast of might in drinking; to entice others to it; to glory in their shame and wickedness — this is a sin that so far exceeds *brutish*, that it becomes *devilish*; and highly provokes the Lord to pour forth his fury upon the places where such sins are committed.

And has not London been guilty of this sin of drunkenness, with the aggravation of it? Have not some of London's *magistrates* been guilty, who should have punished this sin; and too many *ministers*, who should have reproved it both by word and example of sobriety? And for such to be seen drunk and reeling in the streets, was very shameful, and a great provocation. Have not the late judgments in some sort pointed out this sin? The dizziness of head and reeling of people that have been smitten with the plague; the flaming of the heart of the city, and reeling of the houses, and tumbling of them to the ground by the fire — methinks were a reproof of the dizziness and reeling about the streets and houses of such people as had inflamed and distempered themselves with excessive drinking.

16. A sixteenth sin of London is **perverting of justice**. This is a God-provoking sin: "For your hands are stained with blood, your fingers with guilt. Your lips have spoken lies, and your tongue

mutters wicked things. No one calls for justice; no one pleads his case with integrity. They rely on empty arguments and speak lies; they conceive trouble and give birth to evil. So justice is driven back, and righteousness stands at a distance; truth has stumbled in the streets, honesty cannot enter. Truth is nowhere to be found, and whoever shuns evil becomes a prey. The Lord looked and was displeased that there was no justice." Isaiah 59

"Your *rulers* are rebels, companions of thieves; they all love bribes and chase after gifts. They do not defend the cause of the fatherless; the widow's case does not come before them. Therefore the Lord, the Lord Almighty, the Mighty One of Israel, declares: Ah, I will get relief from my foes and avenge myself on my enemies!" Isaiah 1:23-24

I cannot charge London deeply with this sin; not having been myself present much in their courts of judicature; and I would hope that justice has taken place here, as much as in most cities in the world. But when I read what the Lord says concerning Jerusalem, "Go up and down the streets of Jerusalem, look around and consider, search through her squares. If you can find but *one person* who deals honestly and seeks the truth — I will forgive this city!" Jeremiah 5:1. And when withal I consider the dreadful judgments of God upon the city of London, whereby the glory of the magistracy and government of the city is so much stained; I would submit it to inquiry, whether there has not been a failure and perverting of justice in the city? whether bribes and rewards have not blinded the eyes, and the edge of the law has not been turned against well-doers, instead of evil-doers? whether the fatherless and the widow have not been sent weeping to their heavenly Father to complain of injustice? It is not a time to cover faults — but to confess and leave them; least unavoidable ruin come upon us when it will be too late!

17. A seventeenth sin of London is **COVETOUSNESS**. How universally has this sin reigned in the city; so that it may almost be said of London, as it was of Jerusalem, Jeremiah 6. 13, "From the least of them even unto the greatest of them — every one is given to covetousness!" Those who have been free from gluttony, drunkenness, adultery, and the like heinous sins, have on the other hand, addicted themselves to the sin of covetousness. I do not charge all — but O, how almost universal has this sin among tradesmen been; which has evinced itself both in their getting and keeping riches!

(1.) In **getting**. What eager desires after the world, and the obtaining an estate by their trades! What studies and consultations, what racking the brains, and torturing the wits — to find out the best way of thriving in the world! What earnest prosecutions have there been, and laborious endeavors, rising up early, and sitting up late, and wearying the body, and the mind all the day, eating the bread of carefulness, and mingling the drink with worry, crowding up the whole time with worldly business, so that their own health has been disregarded, as well as the worship of God neglected in the families of these worldlings — and all to scrape a little worldly riches together, which some have missed of, notwithstanding all their endeavors. And if they have obtained — yet they have remained more poor in *contentment*, than when they were more poor in their estates. For as their *estates* have increased, so their *desires* have increased, and been farther off from satisfaction; as they have enlarged their shops and trades, and wealth has flowed in upon them — so they have enlarged their *desires* like Hell; and, like the grave, have never said, *It is enough!* When they have added house to house — the more cares and fears, and sometimes piercing sorrows have accompanied their gains; but far have they been from finding the *contentment* and *comfort* in their riches, that they looked for.

(2.) This covetousness has appeared in **keeping** what they have gotten. Keeping, I say, for covetous people have had little heart to spend, though in necessary uses, what they have scraped together. They have had wealth — but the *use* of it they have not had. It has been to them like a treasure in a chest, of which they had lost the key! Or like another man's money in their keeping, which they must not meddle with. Whatever abundance they have had in the bag, and in the coffer — their families have been in need; the table has been penurious, the back and belly have been pinched; they have lived at a poorer rate than those who have been of a poorer income.

The poor might starve at their doors — no pity towards others in want and misery, and the least pity towards themselves. While they have saved, for fear lest *afterwards* they should be in need — they have all along been in need. While they have been saving; and it may be at last they have lost what they have been keeping, to the inexpressible grief, and it may be, breaking of their hearts, which have been so set upon these things!

This sin of covetousness in some, has had deeper rooting; in most, has had too much footing; and in all, has been very heinous and abominable before God. This sin is termed 'idolatry' in Scripture, and the covetous are stigmatized with the name of *idolaters,* Colos. 3:5; Ephesians 5:5. It is *heart-idolatry,* which is forbidden in the first commandment. That thing we make a god to ourselves — which we chiefly desire; if it be the world — then we make the world our god; which is inconsistent with the true love of God the Father, the only true God. 1 John 2:15, "Love not the world, neither the things that are in the world; if any man loves the world — the love of the Father is not in him."

This sin of covetousness is hateful to God and provokes his wrath, "I was enraged by his *sinful greed;* I punished him, and hid my face in anger — yet he kept on in his willful ways!" Isaiah 57:17. Has not God smitten London with the *plague* and fire, among other iniquities, for this iniquity of covetousness?

When London was eagerly pursuing after the world, and all minding and seeking their own interest, without any regard to the interest of God's glory and kingdom, or care of their soul-interest and salvation, which their worldly business would not allow time for — did not the Lord send a *plague,* to put a stop to their trade; and give them time to seek him, and to make their peace with him in their retirements, which they could not, or rather would not find before?

And when they returned with more eagerness to their trades, after the plague was a little over, that they might fetch up, if they could, what they had missed by that intermission — did not the Lord send a *fire* to consume much of that which they had set their hearts upon, and in *large legible letters* write *vanity* upon this *idol,* which so many had worshiped? Let London consider, and lay to heart this sin of covetousness!

18. The eighteenth sin of London is **EXTORTION**. Thus covetousness has expressed itself more grossly in some. I shall not here discourse concerning usury (interest); but the *extorting* use, which some have taken of those who have been in need. The taking of *interest* upon *interest,* and grinding the faces of the poor in their distress, no doubt is a great sin, and very offensive to God. How many extortioners have there been in London, who have enriched themselves — by impoverishing of others; who, "panting after the *dust of the earth* on the head of the poor," have *lent money* to them, not for their help — but to take advantage of them; that so, without mercy, they might take away all that they had, not leaving them so much as a bed to lie on!

Thus some have been like *lions* for cruelty, and like hungry *wolves* unto the poor, "tearing their flesh from their bones, and reserving their very bones to gnaw in the morning," as the Prophet speaks, Zeph. 3:3. This sin of *extortion* was one of the abominations reckoned up by the prophet Ezekiel, for which God was so highly offended with Jerusalem, chapter 22:12; "You take usury and *excessive interest* and make unjust gain from your neighbors by extortion!" For this and other sins there mentioned, it is said, verse 3, "Therefore have I poured out my indignation upon them; I have consumed them with the fire of my wrath!"

Unto this sin of extortion, I may add several other ways, that many in the city have had of getting estates, which some may dispute for the lawfulness of; and because so common and gainful, the sin is little heeded. But when the Lord has been contending with the whole city, and has inflicted a general stroke upon tradesmen, yes, one stroke upon another, and has trodden their trade under his feet, as seeming to be offended with something therein; methinks they should be awakened, and open their eyes, and impartially search, and labor to find out whatever it is that offends him — whatever seeming disadvantage may come to them thereby. And if they will not hearken, God can take away the *remainder*, as he has done a great part, and so force them to a sense of their sin.

One sinful way of getting estates, and, I am persuaded, displeasing to God, is engrossing and *monopolizing* of commodities, which many in London have done, that, having all the commodities of that kind in their hands, they might make their own market, and set their own price upon them; which, if they sold as cheap as otherwise they would do, or as others do when they are shared into many hands, (as possibly some might,) I could not condemn the thing. But when, by getting the *whole* into their hands, they hoist and raise the price beyond the just value, which they necessitate people to give, and that only that they might enrich themselves — this I dare confidently affirm to be unlawful! And my reason is, because hereby they prefer a lesser good, before a greater; namely, the enriching of themselves, and their families, before the more public good of making the commodity more cheap to the commonwealth.

If they say, the injury which the many who buy of it, will sustain, will be very small and inconsiderable; but the good they themselves shall get hereby will be great, and they may be in a better capacity of doing good. I answer, that none ought to do the least injury for the reaping of the greatest advantage — it being absolutely unlawful "to do evil, that good may come thereby, and the damnation of such will be just," Romans 3:6, and consequently a greater injury will come to themselves, than to those whom they injure; yes, the injury will be greater than the good which they obtain.

And as for their being in a capacity of doing more good; I believe that such people, if they do spend such gains, are more forward to spend them on their lusts, than to lay them out in charitable uses! I have not heard that the greatest monopolizers in London have been the most charitable people.

If I were more acquainted with the mysteries of trades in the city, I fear I might find out more than one *mystery of iniquity* among them. If the Lord would put into the hearts of magistrates and citizens to look into trades, and to consider the equity that they bear, and take some course for rectifying abuses in them; it might be one way to obtain a more favorable aspect from Heaven; and the Lord might revive again the trade of London, which now is dying and sinking to the ground.

19. A nineteenth sin of London is **LYING**. It is said of Nineveh, that it was "a city full of lies." Nahum 3:1. O the lies that have been in London! who can reckon them? Lies in the streets; loud lies; false news which we daily hear. Lies in the chambers, secret lies, privy false tales, which are whispered in the ears. Lies in the shop, trading lies, lies told in buying and selling. Mischievous lies, which some tell to do another an injury. We read of some, "that bend their tongue like their bow for lies, who will not speak the truth — but teach their tongue to speak lies," Jeremiah 9:3.

How many liars have there been in London? The children have learned to lie — as soon as they have learned to speak. How have tradesmen been guilty of lying, which some account a necessary adjunct to their trade, without which they could not live! How many laborers have excused themselves, when they have committed faults, with their lies!

But of all lies, *mischievous* lies have been the worst, which some have invented to do an injury to their neighbor; such lies are more immediately begotten by the devil, the father of lies — and such liars are his most genuine offspring. But *all* lies in a sense are mischievous lies; they are mischievous to the party that tells them; even the gossiping liar cannot do so much kindness to his friend by his lie, as he does injury to himself. What! will a man stab himself, to do his friend a courtesy? He who wounds his conscience does worse; he who gains in his trade by his lie, loses more than he gains: a bag of gold is not to be compared with inward peace, and the favor of God (better than life), which, by this sin, is lost.

Surely the Lord, being a God of truth, is much offended with this sin of lying. "God delights," says Solomon, "in those who deal justly; but lying lips are an abomination to him," Proverbs 12. 22. Lying was one sin of Israel, for which "their land did mourn," Hosea 14:2, 3. And God threatens to give "all liars their part in that lake which burns with fire and brimstone," Rev. 21:8. Methinks that one place, should make all liars to tremble. And is not this one sin which some *professors* also in the city have been guilty of, to the shame of their profession; for which the Lord has sent the fire to burn down the city, to awaken us to flee from this sin, as we would escape the future fire of Hell?

20. Another sin of London, is **deception** and **defrauding**. This sin has been the *product of covetousness*, and the *companion of lying*. And how ordinary has it been among tradesmen, which many have been so accustomed to, that it has been as easy to persuade the Ethiopian to change his skin, as to persuade them to leave off their defrauding. This they have looked upon as even essential to their trade, at least as necessary to their gains; yes, some have pleaded a necessity thereof, to get a livelihood for themselves and families. But there is no *necessity* of any *sin*. Duties are necessary — but sins are never necessary. And the gain which is gotten by sin, is like the gain of a garment, which has the plague in it, which, if it brings warmth for the present, quickly also may bring sickness and death. If defrauding brings gain into the purse — it presently brings the plague into the heart, and quickly will bring the pain and punishment of Hell!

To *defraud* another in dealing, is but a more covert way of *stealing*. It is as lawful to steal a purse on the highway, as to steal a shilling by fraud in the shop. The difference lies only in the degree — the nature of the sin, which is theft, is the same in both. And the Lord, as he has expressly forbidden this sin, so he has threatened to avenge it, 1 Thessalonians 4:6. "That no man go beyond or defraud his brother (not only in a *greater* thing but) in *any* matter — because the Lord is the avenger of all such."

The several ways which tradesmen have had of defrauding, would be too large for me to speak of, neither am I so skillful as to understand. The *falsifying of weights and measures* is a heinous sin — a sin practiced among the Jews of old, which God threatens to punish them for, Hosea 12:7. "The merchant uses dishonest scales; he loves to defraud."

And both their sin and God's anger are set forth, "What shall I say about the homes of the wicked filled with treasures gained by cheating? What about the disgusting practice of measuring out grain with dishonest measures? How can I tolerate your merchants who use dishonest scales and weights? The rich among you have become wealthy through extortion and violence. Your citizens are so used to lying that their tongues can no longer tell the truth. Therefore, I have begun to destroy you, to ruin you because of your sins." Micah 6:10-13

And was it not thus with London? Did they not falsify weights and measures, and falsify commodities, and speak falsely concerning the price of them, and take unconscionable gains — and yet profess kind usage of their customers, whom they did most deceive? But if I could, I would not open the cunning ways which some have found out, of defrauding and over-reaching, lest any should learn, and be enticed to practice the sin by the very reproof of it, as I have heard some have done.

Now such people, who have gotten their wealth by defrauding and over-reaching their brethren, bring themselves into such a snare of the devil, that very few ever get out — but are dragged by him thereby into Hell! Because it is not mere *grieving* for this sin, which is necessary to the obtaining of a pardon; but *restitution* is necessary; they must refund, they must restore, either to the parties themselves, or to the poor — what they have gotten wrongfully, if they be able; if not, as much as they have, otherwise they cannot be saved. No salvation came to Zaccheus, until he was resolved upon restitution of what he had wrongfully gained, Luke 19:8. This is one sin which I believe God has smitten London for!

21. The twenty-first sin of London is **PRODIGALITY** and *lavish spending*. Some have spared too much through covetousness, others have spent too much through prodigality. Liberality is a great virtue, and bountiful charity an excellent grace, which London has not been without; but prodigality is a great sin. Thus some have spent above their degree, lavishing out their estates on their tables, on their houses, on their clothes; but the worst prodigality has been, in that which men have lavished out in the satisfaction of their lusts, in drunkenness, gaming, whoring, and the like; and especially those, who have spent profusely that which has been none of their own — but what they have taken up on credit of others, have been most grossly guilty of this sin.

And unto this sin of prodigality and lavish spending — I may refer the sin of excessive mirth and jollity, which has been in London. There is a harmless mirth, which is lawful; and there is a spiritual cheerfulness, which is the duty of Christians; though in times of great sin, and affliction of God's people, sackcloth and mourning befits Christians.

But I am speaking of the mirth of such, who have had the least ground for mirth of any, namely the wicked, unto whom no peace nor joy in that estate, belongs: for them to be so excessively merry, and jovial, and frolic, expressing it in their profane, obscene, and scornful jesting; in their music, singing, and dancing; in their ranting, roaring, and carousing; in many wasteful and lavish ways of spending; when the church is in sackcloth, and lies a bleeding; as too many in London have done: surely God has been offended with this, and has been provoked to send down his judgments, to alter the cheer of London, and hereby to put them into mourning, which they were so averse unto.

Had they foreseen the *plague*, and how many of them would have fallen by it — surely it would have damped their mirth! Had they foreseen the *burning* of the city of London, and that their houses would fall by the fire — surely their laughter would have been turned into heaviness. These judgments they could not foresee; but future judgment, far more dreadful, they might have foreseen, which should have made an impression of sorrow upon them, if possibly by repentance they might avoid and escape it. "Be afflicted, and mourn, and weep, let your laughter be turned into mourning, and your joy into heaviness," James 4:9. Such mourning, if for sin, might be a means to prevent future miseries, and eternal woe and weeping.

Others have reason to mourn for those miseries which will come upon them. "Go to now, you rich men, weep and howl, for the miseries that shall come upon you," James 5:1. But for profane wicked people to sing, and rejoice upon the brink of the grave and Hell — is very unreasonable, and an aggravation of their other sins!

22. The twenty-second sin of London is **ENVYING**. And this sin was to be found not only in *women* — who envied others that exceeded them in beauty of body, in clothes, and dressing, and such like toys; but also in men — who envied those who were of the same trade, who had better houses and shops, more business and wealth, than themselves. Yes, this envying was to be found among many *ministers*, who envied others that had better abilities, and more learning, greater applause, and more auditors than themselves. Envy, besides the great torment that it brings to the heart where it reigns, is a very great provocation to the Lord.

23. The twenty-third sin of London is **SLANDERING** and **BACKBITING**, which has been the consequent of the former. The ninth commandment has been exceedingly broken in London, especially

in a private way of bearing false witness against the neighbor, and wounding his reputation by a slanderous tongue — some inventing lies, and raising slanders, which they have in their consciences known to be false; others taking up *slanders*, readily believing them without any just reproof. This sin you have set forth with a caution to take heed of such people, Jeremiah 9:4, 5.

London has been full of backbiters and tale-bearers, and too many professors have been guilty of this sin; few have entertained backbiters with an angry countenance, which, as the wind drives away rain, would have driven them out of sight.

I might here add the hatred of one another which has been in London (much through slanders), the emulation that has risen from hatred, the wrath that has risen from emulation; and the wrath of God, which has arisen from these and other works of the flesh, spoken of in Galatians 5:19, 20.

24. The twenty-fourth sin of London is **MURMURING**; and that not only in need, and under losses and crosses — but also in fullness and plenty. Many farmers in the country have murmured at the plenty and cheapness of corn; many tradesmen in the city have murmured at the plenty of the commodities which they have dealt in: because, however such plenty is a public and unspeakable mercy — yet they have had the less private advantage, which has been chiefly regarded by them.

Yes, some, in their murmurings have wished for a *plague*, that the survivors might have the better trade; and I have heard that a *fire*, also had been wished for, to take off the plenty of such commodities, that the remainder might bear the higher rate. Is it a wonder, then, if God have sent *plague* and *fire*, which some have called for by such murmuring speeches? The Israelites in the wilderness were plagued for their murmuring; and the murmuring company of Korah, which were not swallowed up with him, were consumed by a fire from Heaven.

25. The twenty-fifth and last sin of London which I shall speak of, is **CARNAL SECURITY**, another of Sodom's sins. It is said of the Sodomites, Luke 17:28, 29. "It was the same in the days of Lot. People were eating and drinking, buying and selling, planting and building. But the day Lot left Sodom, fire and sulfur rained down from heaven and destroyed them all." When London had provoked God so highly by so many sins — yet how secure were they before his judgments broke forth upon them — they ate and drank, they bought and sold, etc. They sat at ease, and put far from them the evil day; as, Amos 6:1, 3; they were quiet and at rest, little expect-

ing such changes as have come upon them, and took little care to prevent them. They were secure and trusted in arms of flesh, broken reeds, which have always failed.

And I might add here, as a cause of the security of some, the presumptuous confidences of future events, which belong only to God to foreknow, which some have taken upon them so absolutely to determine, as if they had looked into the book of God's decrees, or had an infallible revelation from him of what would come to pass. O the good days that some have looked for, upon presumption of what they had no ground for. Great expectations many had of the fall of *Antichrist* and *Babylon* in the year 1666; and other events, limiting times, which God has not clearly revealed, which is an entrenching upon God's prerogative, and I believe a greater provocation than such people are aware of. This may be one reason why London is fallen instead of *Babylon*, in this year of such expectation and presumption.

By this time, it may be, the reader may be wearied with reading, as I am with thinking and writing of **London's sins**. But how has the Lord been wearied with the bearing of them! How has he been pressed with the weight of them, as a cart is pressed that is full of sheaves! Amos 2:13. If, when you have read of London *judgments*, and you consider London's *provocations* — you must needs acknowledge that God is righteous, in that he has punished London no more than they have deserved for these sins!

# Section 9

God's righteousness will further appear, if we consider that **he has punished London *less* than her iniquities deserved**. God might have punished London deservedly with more dreadful judgments — both in the same, and another kind.

**1. God might have deservedly punished London *worse* in the same kind.**

1. In the judgment of the **PLAGUE**. It was a dreadful plague indeed; but God could have made it *more dreadful.* Where he shot one arrow — he might have shot an hundred. He visited many families — he might have visited every family, and swept away every house with the broom of destruction. Though so many fell — yet I believe that five parts in six of the inhabitants of London were preserved. God might have taken away the five parts, and have left but one alive; yes, it might have been said of London, as it was of Israel, "The virgin Israel has fallen, never to rise again! She lies abandoned on the ground, with no one to help her up!" Amos 5:2.

God might have trebled the hundreds that died by the plague; he might have sent out his arrows after *all* the inhabitants of London that were gone into the country, and smitten them wherever he found them; or he might have met with them upon their return home, and given commission to *Death* to lay hold on them as soon as they entered into their doors. He might have depopulated the city of London by the plague — so that *every* house should have had dead corpses lying, and none to bury them. He might have made our plague astonishing, fearful, and of long continuance.

We who have survived so great a mortality, have reason to say, that *deservedly* it might have been greater; that we deserved as much or more to fall for our more heinous sins, than thousands that are gone down into the pit! Surely "it is of the Lord's mercies that we are not consumed!" He was merciful in *sparing* of us; he would have been righteous if he had *destroyed* us.

Think with yourselves: you that are alive, and remain escaped. How fearful would the plague have been — if it had come home to your houses! You were afraid to hear of *others'* houses plagued and shut up, what would you have been if it had entered *your* doors? You were afraid when others were struck with the disease — what would you have been if you had been struck yourselves?

Lost sinners, what would you have done if the plague arrow had pierced through your livers; if, under such guilt and wrath — you had been smitten? When you had such a *plague of sin in your hearts* — that you should have had the plague of pestilence in your bodies! When you were so rotten and corrupt, and defiled inwardly — that you should have boils, and ulcers, and running sores outwardly! When conscience was so filled with guilt — that your bodies should have been filled with this disease! In a word, if, when you had the marks of *Hell* and *damnation* in your *souls* — that you should have had the marks of inevitable death in your *bodies!* O the dread that would have seized upon you!

The judgment of the plague might have been worse to you! You might have spent more than a year in Hell by this time — among devils and damned spirits! You might by this time have been inured to those *torments* which you could not have endured — but must have endured, without any possibility of deliverance forever!

Many of you who have escaped, have your families *broken* by death — when other *whole* families are swept away. Suppose your dear wife had fallen, or your hopeful children had been nipped by death in the very bud, and your families had been maimed — the judgment would have been much sorer on you. None can say but God might have righteously punished London more severely by the plague!

(2.) God might have punished London also more severely by the **FIRE**. The greatest part of the city is fallen — it might have been the whole. Most of the city within the walls is consumed — the flames might have issued forth at all the gates, and consumed all the suburbs too. All the *goods* might have been burnt with the houses, and all the *inhabitants* with the *habitations*.

The fire, though it burned dreadfully — yet it began at one end, and came on so slowly, that most of the inhabitants of London had time to remove themselves and the choicest of their goods; some livelihood was left, and materials for a future trade.

Suppose the fire had been so sudden, or had been kindled in so many places, that there had been no possibility of removing anything, except the people themselves. Suppose all the silver, and gold, and riches of the city had been melted by this fire; that all the wares and merchandise, all the garments, beds, and household goods had been turned into ashes, and many thousand families that had been turned out of house, had been turned out of all, and quite bereaved of all their substance, so that nothing had remained to them for necessary use — this would have been very sore indeed!

Alas! what would they have done? Where would they have gone for relief? Would the court have supplied them? Could the country have helped and maintained so many, when so much impoverished themselves, that in many places they are hardly able to live? Could they have hoped for relief from foreign nations? Are not all the world almost our enemies? Is charity so warm abroad? Alas! what would they have done? Must not many of them have pined away in their needs, and starved under hedges, for lack of suitable provisions? This would have been dreadful indeed!

Or suppose they had lugged their goods out of London from the fire, and the whole city had been burnt down with all the suburbs, and no habitations left standing hereabouts; what would they have done with their goods? where would they have disposed of them? How could they have continued their trades? How could they have lived this cold winter season? Could they have struck up booths presently, fit for themselves to abide in, which would have sheltered them from the injury of the weather? Where would they have had materials, when all was burnt?

What would they have done? must not their goods have been spoiled, by lying abroad? would not they themselves, who had been used to so much tenderness, have quickly grown sick, and died in the fields? would not thousands have starved for cold? and what provisions could they have had for food and other necessaries? Besides, would they not have been a prey to thieves and cut-throats? Would not many of their enemies, who laughed at the fall of the city, have rejoiced much more, and taken advantage to come upon them in their nakedness, and butchered them without mercy.

But, suppose the fire that begun at one corner, had been kindled in every gate at the same time, when all the inhabitants had been asleep in their houses, and they had been inclosed with flames, and no possibility of escape — how dreadful would the fire have been then? If, when they awakened in the morning, they had seen the smoke ascending round about them, and the fire drawing near to them; if both ends of a street had been on fire together, and they in the midst, and had heard, with the roaring of the fire, a greater roaring of the people who were burning with the houses: O the rueful looks! Oh the horrible shrieks by women and children! Oh the dreadful amazement and perplexity which would have been in such a place and case!

To be burnt alive, is dreadful; but think what tortures would have been in the spirits of guilty sinners, who had not made their peace with God, that had slept out the harvest and day of grace, who had made no provision for death and eternity! The noise and roaring without — would have been nothing to the lashes and tearings within them; the fire in their houses would have been but small — in comparison of the fire in their consciences, and the flames of Hell-fire, which, if awakened, they would have seen just before them.

This judgment of the fire might have been more dreadful than it was; people are escaped; goods and wealth much saved; houses standing to receive them; trade going on: God might have punished London more sorely in the same kind.

**2. God might have punished London more severely in other kinds of judgments.**

(1.) He might have brought upon them, and upon the whole land, the sword of a foreign **enemy**, as he did upon Jerusalem, and the land of Judea, for their sins; which being so pathetically set forth by the prophet Jeremiah, I shall represent to the eye: "A besieging army is coming from a distant land, raising a war cry against the cities of Judah. They surround her like men guarding a field, because she has rebelled against me," declares the Lord. "Your own conduct and actions have brought this upon you. This is your punishment. How bitter it is! How it pierces to the heart!" Oh, my anguish, my anguish! I writhe in pain. Oh, the agony of my heart! My heart pounds within me, I cannot keep silent. Disaster follows disaster; the whole land lies in ruins. In an instant my tents are destroyed, my shelter in a moment. I looked at the earth, and it was formless and empty; and at the heavens, and their light was gone. I looked at the mountains, and they were quaking; all the hills were swaying. I looked, and there were no people; every bird in the sky had flown away. I looked, and the fruitful land was a desert; all its towns lay in ruins before the Lord, before his fierce anger. At the sound of horsemen and archers every town takes to flight. Some go into the thickets; some climb up among the rocks. All the towns are deserted; no one lives in them." Jeremiah 4

This might have been the judgment, and these the complaints of London and England, which would have been worse than plague or *fire*. The *plague* reached many — but the *sword* might have reached all; the fire devoured houses — but the sword might have devoured the inhabitants. The Lord might have brought a foreign sword, and open invasion; or he might have given up London to a more private, sudden butchery and massacre by the hands of cruel Papists, as was feared; which would have been more dreadful than the massacre of the Protestants by the Papists in Paris; because our numbers do so far exceed those which were in that city.

If bloody Papists had come into our houses in the dead of the night, with knives in their hands; and having set watch at every street's end, had allowed none to escape — but cruelly slaughtered the husband with the wife, the parents and the children together, ripping up women with child, and not sparing either silver hairs, or the sucking babe; if there had been a cry at midnight, "They are come!" but no possibility of flying from them, or making resistance against them; if, instead of heaps of stones and bricks in the top of every street, there had been heaps of dead bodies and ran down with gore-blood; surely this judgment would have been more dreadful than the plague or fire, which have been among us.

(2.) God might have punished London with **famine**, which is a greater judgment than the plague or sword; if the Lord had taken away the whole staff of bread, and cut off all provisions of food from the many thousand souls that lived in and about the city; how dreadful would this have been! If a famine had been so sore in London, that people would have been forced to eat one another, and their own flesh, as it was in "Samaria and Jerusalem;" if, instead of houses in London, God should have made the people as fuel of the fire in this judgment, as is threatened, Isaiah 9:19, 20. "By the wrath of the Lord Almighty the land will be scorched and the people will be fuel for the fire; no one will spare his brother. On the right they will devour, but still be hungry; on the left they will eat, but not be satisfied. Each will feed on the flesh of his own offspring." If London had been forced through hunger to eat the flesh of their own arms, and the fruit of their own bodies, oh what dismal faces would there have been in the city? In the inconceivable pain of gnawing hunger — how would death have been chosen rather than life! Those which die by the plague, or are slain by the sword, would be counted happy in comparison with those who live under such a judgment.

Lastly, the righteousness of God in the judgments he has inflicted on London, appears, in that he might, instead of plague and fire on earth, have punished them with the plagues and fires of Hell; which such sins as we have reckoned up, have abundantly deserved. Tyre and Sidon now in Hell; Sodom and Gomorrah under the vengeance of eternal fire, were not guilty of such sins as London was guilty of!

And what are body-plagues here — in comparison of soul-plagues hereafter? What is a fire that burns down a city — in comparison with the fire of Hell, which shall burn the damned, and never be quenched!

God has punished London no more than her iniquities have deserved; God has punished London *less* than her iniquities have deserved: therefore, in speaking most terribly, he has answered most righteously.

# Section 10

## Concerning the DESIGN of these judgments

What does God mean by this *terrible voice?* by speaking such terrible things in the city of London?

The Lord has not only *spoken* — but *cried* and *shouted*; he has lifted up his voice like a trumpet, and his voice has not been inarticulate and insignificant — but has had a meaning; and those who have an ear to hear, may understand; for as the voice of the Lord has cried *in* the city, so the voice of the Lord has cried *to* the city, "Listen! The Lord's voice cries unto the city! The man of wisdom shall see your name. Hear the rod, and the One who has appointed it!" Micah 6:9

Some take notice of the judgments themselves, and the effects of them upon *themselves* and their families. They discourse of the *plague* and how many died thereby, that they have lost such a relation, such a friend or neighbor was visited, and died quickly. They discourse of the *fire*, where it began, how it increased and prevailed, what day such a street fell, and where their houses were consumed; what they lost, and how much they saved. And it may be, some speak of the hands of *men*, who were suspected to enkindle and carry it on. But few discourse of the *hand of God*, which sent both plague and fire, and what he means by such strange and dreadful judgments. But "the man of wisdom," such as are wise consider that these judgments do not spring out of the dust — but were sent down from the God of Heaven! They see God's name, and God's hand, which has been stretched forth upon London. They know that both *plague* and fire have had their commission from the God of Heaven — otherwise they could not have wrought with such force and power.

They see God's "name," that is, the glorious attributes of his name displayed. God proclaimed his name, before Moses, when he caused his goodness to pass before him, and discovered himself to be "the Lord, the Lord God; gracious and merciful, slow to anger, abundant in loving kindness, goodness, and truth," Exodus 34. 6. And God has proclaimed his name before London, in causing his judgments to come upon the city, and has declared himself to be "the Lord, the Lord God, holy and jealous, a God that can be angry when much provoked, and yet righteous in the severest judgments which He inflicts!"

A man of wisdom may see God's name in London's judgments; and as he may see power and righteousness in God's name, so he may see grace and goodness in the name of God, which has passed before the city; he may see and know that God has a gracious meaning and design of good to London in these judgments; he may see God's name, and hear God's voice, and what it is, that he speaks by the rod.

Oh that London were thus wise! that they would open their eyes and see God's name! That they would see God's hand — so just and righteous; as also that they would open their *ears*, and hear God's voice, and understand God's design — so gracious and so much for their good! O that God would open the ears of London, and bend them to the discipline of his judgments! that with the loss of friends and relations by the *plague*, and of houses and goods by the *fire* — they may not lose the good of these judgments too, though of another mind — yet of far greater value, which God intends them.

The inquiry then is — what does the Lord mean by the *plague* and by the *fire* in the city? What does he call for by this terrible voice, and look for in London, that these judgments may turn to their advantage?

# Section 11

## The DUTIES which God expects from London after such desolations by the Plague and Fire, are these:

**1. God expects that London should AWAKE.** London has been asleep; both the foolish and the wise virgins have been asleep; and when such a voice has come down in these judgments, which have been revealed from Heaven, crying in the midnight of their carnal security, "Behold, the great God is come forth from his place, and is entered into London in fury!" — surely all should awake and arise, and prepare to *meet* him, seeing none can *flee* from him. God has seemed to be asleep, while he exercised so much *patience* towards London. His arm slept in his bosom; but now the Lord has been awakened with the loud cry of England and London's sins; his arm has awaked, and put on strength and vengeance.

Awake! then, O London, awake! open your **eyes**. Draw open your curtains; come forth from your bed; look out of your windows! Apparitions! apparations! strange sights to be seen. Behold! Heaven is opened, and God is come down upon earth, clothed with garments of lightning! God is come down in his majesty, and looks upon London with a terrible countenance! Behold the amazing terror of God in the late strange and prodigious judgments. What! do you not see him? Surely you are fast asleep still! Your eyes are closed — the veil is over them!

Awake! London, awake! open your **ears**. Hearken! O the *trumpet* that has been sounding from Heaven over the city is exceeding loud! O the thunderings of the terrible voice of the angry God! the voice of the Lord has been powerful and very dreadful. What! can you sleep under such a noise? Surely you are dead asleep, dead in sin and carnal security. What will awaken you — if the judgments do not awaken you? If a shrill and loud trumpet does not pierce your ears — will soft music enter? If the sound of *cannons* are not heard — can any expect that *pistols* should? If, when the lion roars in your ears you can sleep still — will soft whispers awaken you? What will awaken you — if the loud voice of these divine judgments does not awaken you? The Lord called upon you before by his ministers, by his mercies — now he has shouted in your ears by his solemn judgments!

Awake! London, awake! You have been roused out of your habitations; methinks you should be roused out of your carnal security. What! sleep when *dying!* dying by the plague, and tumbling into the grave! What! sleep when *burning!* burning by the fire, and tumbling into desolation! What! sleep in a *storm!* when winds are blowing, and waves roaring, sea filling, and ship sinking!

"What do you mean, O sleeper!" — could the heathen ship-master say, in such a case, unto Jonah, chapter 1:5, 6, when he lay fast asleep in the ship, in the midst of the devouring storm. "How can you sleep at a time like this? Get up and pray to your God! Perhaps he will pay attention to us and spare our lives!" And may not I say, "What do you mean, O sleepy London! Have you not perceived the *storm* that has beaten so fiercely on your head? Do you not perceive that your ship is shattered and broken, and the sea is filling it — and you are in danger of sinking, and that quickly, unless some speedy course is taken for prevention? And yet can you sleep still? Awake! Arise! Call upon your God! Perhaps he will pay attention to us and spare our lives!"

God calls upon sleepy sinners to awake!

Suppose you were under the power of *cruel enemies*, who had killed your husbands, or wives, or dear children and friends — and you knew not how soon they might fall upon *you*, and cut your throats! Could you sleep securely in the same house with such people?

Just so, you are under the power of *tyrannical lusts*, which are far worse enemies! You are under the reigning power of sin, which has brought the plague into the city, and whereby some of you have been deprived of these relations, and you know not how soon sin may bring death upon yourselves, not only the first death — but the second death! Not only temporal death — but eternal death; and deprive you not only of life — but happiness, and all hopes of the least share in it forever. And yet, can you sleep securely with *sin* in your hearts — with such an enemy, with such a viper, in your bosoms?

When the fire was in London, I believe few of you could take much sleep! When the fire was burning in your streets, and burning down your houses — you could not sleep in your houses, lest the fire would have burned you and your family too!

Just so, when the *fire of lust* is *within* you, and burning within you; when the fire of God's anger is kindled *above* you, and burning over you; and the fire of Hell, so dreadful and unextinguishable, is burning *beneath* you; and you are hanging over the burning lake of fire by a twine-thread, which, before long, will untwine of itself — and may, before you are aware, and suddenly, be cut or snapped asunder — and then you must drop into the midst of flames!

Can you sleep under the guilt and power of sin — when you are in such danger?

Awake! sinners, awake! God does not burn you now — but *warns* you first! He burns your *houses*, that you might awake, and escape a more dreadful fire! Awake! sinners — when will you awake! how *often*, how *long*, how *loud* shall God call upon you — before you will arise? "Awake you that sleep, and arise from the dead, and Jesus Christ shall give you life." Ephesians 5:14

"A little sleep, a little slumber, a little folding of the hands to rest." What! can you continue to sleep now? Was not this your tone long ago, when you were under the calls of the *Word* — and is it the same under the *rod* too? What will awaken you? When do you think you shall be awakened — if still you lie down in the bed of carnal security, and love to slumber upon the lap of pleasure, and after a little startle, sleep faster than before?

*Ministers* have preached, and you have slept under their sermons; but when *God* has preached, methinks you should awake! When Paul preached to Felix a sermon of judgment — Felix trembled. God has preached one, nay, *two sermons of judgment*, and that more feelingly than Paul could! Methinks you should awake, and not drop asleep so soon, because God gives you a little respite to learn his sermon, before he preach the *third* sermon, which may be your last and eternally ruining sermon! If you do not awake by the sound of his judgments *before* you, you shall awake by the sense of his judgments *upon* you! If the *plague* and *fire* of London do not awaken you — you shall be awakened by the plagues and fire of Hell, which you shall see and feel — but not be able to flee from, as here you might do, if presently awakened.

God calls upon *sleepy* ***sinners*** to awake — and God calls upon *drowsy* ***saints*** to awake — and was there not great need? Were not the *Jonahs* gone down into the bottom of the ship, and lying on pillows? Were not the *wise virgins* turning foolish, sleeping with the rest, untrimmed and undressed? Had there not of late a strange *torpor* and *stupidity* seized upon the spirits of God's own people? Was not the ancient vigor and activity, which once they had in the ways of worship of God — much abated and decayed before these judgments came upon London.

Awake, then, you drowsy saints, awake! See your nakedness.

Put on your garments which you have laid aside; shake yourselves from the dust which has covered and sullied your faces, and loosen the bands of sleep. God has been thundering, your Father has been angry, and displeased with you as well as with others. Your God has spoken in his jealousy, and he has spoken in his fury; he has spoken with a loud voice in righteousness and in judgment.

*God's children* — Awake! Your Father is stirring, and knocking, and calling; yes, he has entered your chamber, and smitten you on this side and that — and yet will you not arise! He has been crying in your ears — now he is looking and hearkening whether you will cry in his, and what you will say and do for the prevention of the ruin of England, which he seems to be threatening. It is high time to awake out of sleep — for now is the utter destruction of the city and nation nearer, it may be, than you believe or imagine.

Awake, then, put off your clothes of night and darkness, in which you have been sleeping, and put on your garments of light! Clothe yourselves with humility, and begirt yourself with all your graces, and get to God's knee, hang about his arm, put yourselves in the breach, "Perhaps he will pay attention to us and spare our lives!"

**2. The Lord now, after his speaking by terrible things — expect that London should stand in AWE of him.** God's judgments made this impression upon *David*, "I tremble in awe of You; I fear Your judgments!" Psalm 119:120. And see how the prophet Habakkuk behaved himself, when God spoke with a terrible voice, "O Lord, have heard all about you, Lord. I am filled with awe by your amazing works!" Habakkuk 3:2.

"I see God moving across the deserts from Edom, the Holy One coming from Mount Paran. His brilliant splendor fills the heavens, and the earth is filled with his praise. His coming is as brilliant as the sunrise. Rays of light flash from his hands, where his awesome power is hidden. Pestilence marches before him; plague follows close behind. When he stops — the earth shakes. When he looks — the nations tremble. He shatters the everlasting mountains and levels the eternal hills. He is the Eternal One! I see the people of Cushan in distress, and the nation of Midian trembling in terror. Was it in anger, Lord, that you struck the rivers and parted the sea? Were you displeased with them? You brandished your bow and your quiver of arrows. You split open the earth with flowing rivers. The mountains watched and trembled. Onward swept the raging waters. The mighty deep cried out, lifting its hands to the Lord. The sun and moon stood still in the sky as your brilliant arrows flew and your glittering spear flashed. You marched across the land in anger and trampled the nations in your fury!" Habakkuk 3.

When the pestilence has gone before him, and burning coals at his feet; when the Lord drove London asunder, scattered the inhabitants, and made the stately buildings to bow and fall, whose rearings up none can remember; when the tents of London have been in affliction, and the curtains of city have trembled: when death had been riding upon horses, and his bow has been made quite naked; when the Heavens have been astonished at God's judgments, and the sun and moon have hid their heads in their habitations at the shining of his glittering spear; when the Lord has marched through the city in his indignation, has wounded the heads of so many wicked with his arrows, and struck through so many habitations with his staves. Oh! how London should tremble and quiver — and stand in *awe* of this glorious Majesty, at the voice of these terrible judgments!

Read, and apply what the Lord speaks by the prophet Isaiah, "Listen to what I have done, you nations far away! And you that are near, acknowledge my might! The sinners in Jerusalem shake with fear. Terror seizes the godless. 'Who can live with this devouring fire?' they cry. 'Who can survive this all-consuming fire?' In your thoughts, you will ponder the former terror." Isaiah 33:13, 14, 18.

Methinks the sinners now in London should be afraid, and fearfulness should surprise the hypocrites; when God has sent so many of their number into the *everlasting burnings of Hell* by the *plague*, and by such a devouring *fire* has consumed so many habitations!

Tremble, you sinners, at this — and be you horribly afraid, all you workers of iniquity! God has come down with a shout, the Lord with the sound of a trumpet. He has taken his weapons in his hand, and has appeared in London as a furious enemy! Should not this make the sinners in the city to quake, and strike a dread upon the spirits of the rebellious? When the Lord has spoken thus, and done thus, because of our sins, should not London, yes, all England, "hear and fear, and no more behave so wickedly."

Because God was patient formerly, you presumed, "When the sentence for a crime is not quickly carried out, the hearts of the people are filled with schemes to do wrong!" Ecclesiastes 8:11. Therefore your hearts were hardened and resolved in your evil ways. "Because the Lord kept silence — you thought he was altogether such a one as yourselves!" Psalms 50:21. You thought, it may be, that he took no more notice of you — than you did of him, or that you had no more reason to fear him — than he had to fear you!

You thought, it may be, that God had forsaken the earth, or had hidden his face — and would never see your wickedness. And oh, how *bold* have you been, how *audacious* and *fearless* in sin! You were afraid to offend *man*, though a *worm* — and yet you have not been afraid to offend God, the great King of the whole world! *Men's* laws have kept you from sins — but the laws of God have not put upon you the least restraint. You have lived and sinned as if there were no God; or as if he had been so gentle, and mild, and merciful — that you might do any affront to him, and he not be displeased with you; or, as if though he were displeased — yet his displeasure were not to be regarded, and that he had *no power* to execute vengeance upon you!

But now God's *patience* has, in a great measure, been turned into *fury!* Now, sinners, you may perceive a little, that *God can be angry!* And when his anger is kindled but a little, if it does express itself so dreadfully — what dreadful expressions will there be of it, when it breaks forth into an open flame? If his anger is such in the day of some lighter, temporal judgments — then what will it be in the day of the unveiling of the *storehouses* of it upon all the wicked — at the glorious appearing of our great God and Savior, Jesus Christ!

But God's vengeance now in these judgments should work your hearts to a *fear* and *awe* of this righteous Judge, who has done such solemn executions in the city! It should bridle and keep you from that fearless course of sin, in which you were rushing, as the horse rushes into the battle.

When *Balaam's donkey* saw the *angel* stand in the way with a drawn sword — he was afraid, and would not go forward, though spurred on, and beaten by his master. And when God stands in the way with his sword of judgment, which has made such slaughter already, and is lifted up again to strike you — methinks you should be afraid and turn back! It is the *way to Hell* that God stands in by his judgments — and will you break through all into those flames? Oh stand in awe, and sin not, commune with your own hearts. Consider what has been doing in London, and who has done these things. You have nearly escaped, it may be, with your lives; oh learn to fear the glorious and fearful name of the Lord God in these dreadful judgments.

And as God expects that the *world* and his *enemies* should stand in awe of him — so also much more, that *his people* should. Some, it may be, when God gave them free access to him, and admitted unto familiarity with him, and encouraged them to boldness and confidence, and strewed their path with nothing but mercies — such might abuse his goodness, and forget to mingle faith and love with due reverence and fear — and begin to be too overbold with God, and did not consider their vile sinfulness — but forgot the severity which they deserved for sin. Therefore God appears in the way of these judgments with such terrible rebukes — that his own people might be brought unto a due awe and fear of his name; that, if they *love* him — they may *fear* him too; if they pray with *boldness* — they may pray also with *reverence*; if they rejoice in his goodness — they may tremble also at his judgments.

**3. God expects that London should now SEARCH and TRY THEIR WAYS.** When God had punished *Jerusalem* with dreadful judgments, in the lamentation of which the prophet Jeremiah writes a book, see what use and improvement he calls upon the people to make hereof, Lamentations 3:40, "Let us *search and try our ways* — and turn again unto the Lord." This was the practice of David m the day of his trouble, Psalm 77:6. "I communed with mine own heart, and my spirit made *diligent search.*"

It has been a *day of God's wrath* in London, as it was in Jerusalem, "a day of wrath, a day of distress and anguish, a day of trouble and ruin, a day of darkness and gloom, a day of clouds and blackness," Zeph. 1:15. There have been dark and thick clouds over London, which in part have broken into dreadful storms, and amazing tempests of God's anger, expressed in the late judgments! And all have been the product of London's sins, which may yet produce far worse effects. London is thereby called upon with a loud voice — to search and find out those sins which have been the *troublers* of the city.

I suppose that true citizens would be forward to search after those people that had a hand in the first kindling and carrying on the fire, which burned their habitations to the ground. Allow me to make a revealing of *London's arsonists* — how you may find the people, how you may trace their footsteps, what marks they bear, what their names are, and where their abide! I need not lead you far in the search. The sinners, the *sinners of London* — kindled the fire of London! It was sin which set the first house on fire — and sin was like gas poured upon the flames, which put such fury unto them, that none could withstand until the greatest part of the city was fallen and turned into ashes!

The swearers, the adulterers, the drunkards, the unrighteous, the profane, and the like sinners — have been London's arsonists, and had a hand in pulling down this and other judgments upon the place where they lived! And is it hard to find out these people? Have they gone far from the place of their former abode? The skirts of London are remaining, and if you turn up the skirts, or turn your eye under them, and look into the houses standing about the city — may you not find many of these people, these vile sinners inhabiting, who are still *blowing hard at the fire of God's anger;* and pulling hard with cords of vanity and sin, for further judgments?

Search, London — search, and find out your enemies, your destroyers! Have not you destroyed yourself? Search, and find out your *sins,* which have brought such disaster and ruins upon you!

Sinners, enter into your closets, retire into yourselves, take the candle of the Lord, and look into your inner rooms; make a strict search into your hearts, find out those *filthy lusts* which lodge in dark corners, and bring them forth to be slain! Read over the old records of your lives, consult the register of your consciences, revolve in your minds, your former sins. Take the looking-glass of the Word — and look upon *your faces* in it, and see how many *spots* it will reveal, which you never before perceived; not beauty-spots — but spots of deformity, plague-spots, death-marks, Hell-tokens — such as will bring upon you inevitable and eternal misery, unless they are wiped off! Take the *rule of the Word,* and measure *your actions* by it, and you may quickly perceive how much they have fallen short, how crooked they have been! Compare your *actions,* with the straight rule of God's law, and you may find out many irregularities!

If you do not find out your sins — then your sins will find you out, and God's judgments will find you out! And if you are found out in your sins — woe be unto you! O the horror which will be upon your consciences, when ruining judgments are inflicted upon you particularly, and you cannot escape; when *death* looks you in the face, and comes with the *sting of sin in its mouth* to devour you. But, O the horror you will be under *hereafter* — if you are taken away in your sins; when your souls shall be summoned, immediately after their separation, unto the judgment-bar of God, where you will be searched, and tried, and condemned to everlasting torment, by an inevitable and irreversible sentence of the Judge himself!

O therefore hearken to the voice of God in these *temporal* judgments on the city, (after which you still remain alive, through infinite patience) which calls upon you to search and try your ways — that you may escape more fearful judgments which God may be preparing for you! Labor to find out *your sins*, which are the cause of all judgments — temporal and eternal.

And to help you in your search after sin, read the *catalogue* I have already given you of *London's sins*, and examine yourselves thereby. Be very serious, and thorough, and impartial, in this search; sequester yourselves often from all company; ease your mind of the load of worldly business. Strive against temptations and indispositions to the work; set yourselves in the presence of the heart-searching God; beg the help of his Spirit to reveal to you what has displeased and provoked him. Search after sin . . .

as offensive to God,
as destructive to yourselves,
as your worst enemy,
as the cause of plague and fire in London, and
as that which will bring the plagues and fire of Hell upon you — if it is not found out and subdued!

**4. God expects that London should ACKNOWLEDGE THEIR SINS unto him.** When the Prophet had directed the people to search and try their ways, after the execution of such judgments upon them, Lam. 3:40, see the following direction, verses 41, 42. "Let us lift up our hearts and our hands to God in heaven, and say: We have sinned and rebelled" etc. Thus the prophet confesses the sins of Jerusalem, 1:8, 9, "Jerusalem has sinned greatly and so has become unclean. All who honored her despise her, for they have seen her nakedness; she herself groans and turns away. Her filthiness clung to her skirts; she did not consider her future. Her fall was astounding; there was none to comfort her!"

And; thus the daughter of Zion, as she bewails her affliction, so she acknowledges her transgression, Jerusalem reaches out for help, but no one comforts her. Regarding his people Israel, the Lord has said, 'Let their neighbors be their enemies! Let them be thrown away like a filthy rag!' 'The Lord is right,' Jerusalem says, 'for I rebelled against him! Lord, see my anguish! My heart is broken and my soul despairs, for I have rebelled against you. In the streets the sword kills, and at home there is only death!'" Lamentations 1:17-20

Thus Daniel, after dreadful judgments, makes a confession of the sins of the people of Israel, "I prayed to the Lord my God and confessed: O Lord, you are a great and awesome God! You always fulfill your covenant and keep your promises of unfailing love to those who love you and obey your commands. But we have sinned and done wrong. We have rebelled against you and scorned your commands and regulations. We have refused to listen to your servants the prophets, who spoke on your authority to our kings and princes and ancestors and to all the people of the land. Lord, you are in the right; but as you see, our faces are covered with shame!" Daniel 9:4-7

And verse 11, 12. "All Israel has disobeyed your instruction and turned away, refusing to listen to your voice. So now the solemn curses and judgments written in the Law of Moses, the servant of God, have been poured down on us because of our sin! You have kept your word and done to us and our rulers exactly as you warned. Never has there been such a disaster as happened in Jerusalem!"

God expects that London should *find out* their sins, and having found them, that they should make *confession* of them. O that the profane and ungodly generation in London, whose sins have been enumerated in the previous catalogue, would be persuaded to get alone by themselves, and consider their evil ways, and what the consequence of their sins have been in bringing down *temporal* judgments; and what the consequence of their sins is likely to be, even the bringing upon them *eternal* judgments, and that they would fall down and prostrate themselves at God's foot, and covering their cheeks with shame and blushing, because of their filthiness and foul sins under the view of so holy an eye; that they would acknowledge their transgressions unto him, not only in general — but also particularly, with their heinous aggravations!

O that with an inward deep sense, with a bleeding, broken heart, they would fill their mouths with confession; that they would take to themselves words, and say,

"We have rebelled against you, O Lord, and done wickedly, and grievously offended you! We have been foolish, and ignorant of you. We have been *worse than beasts* before you: the ox acknowledges his owner, and the donkey his master; but, though we are your creatures, and live upon your bounty — yet we have not acknowledged you, and have had less consideration than those beasts which have had no reason! We have been sinful people, laden with iniquity, a seed of evil doers! We have been corrupters of others. We have forsaken you, and by our wickedness provoked you to anger. We have been stubborn and disobedient, serving your enemies — the devil and our own lusts!

"We have neglected, yes, refused to serve and worship you in our families and closets — living as if there had been *no God* in the world. We have seldom, if ever, taken your name into our mouths, unless it has been in vain, unless in our oaths and curses. We have defiled your ordinances, and have often been more wicked on the Lord's-day, than any day of the week besides. When we were children, we disobeyed our parents — but we have disobeyed you much more, who commanded us to honor them. When we were children in years, we were full grown in sin! When we were weak in body — we were strong in heart to commit iniquity! We learned the *trade of sin* before any other, and were *clever scholars in the school of the devil* — when dull and blockish to learn anything which was good! We were wise to do evil — when to do good we had no understanding! Our *iniquities* have increased over our heads, faster than our *years* have done!

"Since we have been governors of others, we have had no government upon our own spirits, and have endeavored to lead those under our charge — with us in the way to Hell, instead of laboring to draw them into the way of Heaven, by our example, command and persuasions! We have filled up all our relations with sin, instead of filling them up with Christian duty. If we have not murdered any with our hand, we have murdered many with our tongue; swords have been in our lips, and bitter reviling speeches in our mouths; heart-murder we have been guilty of. O the inordinate *anger* that has boiled in our hearts! O the *envy* and *malice* which have gnawed our spirits, and been working daily within us!

"And especially those people have been most hated by us, who have had your image upon them, and have been best beloved by you — we have scorned them, and looked upon them as despicable people! We have separated them from our company, as those who dampen and spoil our mirth by their words and looks of reproof. Yes, we have even persecuted them, as seditious and factious people; when in truth, it was their *holiness* and *pure lifestyle* which contradicts and condemns our wicked practices, which stirred up our anger against them. We have scoffed at them — who have prayed for us! Because of our lusts, we have looked upon them, and dealt with them as our enemies — who were the best friends to our souls, and above all things desired our salvation.

"You have given us grain, and wine, and oil, and plentiful provisions for our body — but we have abused your mercies by our intemperance and luxury! We have been guilty of drunkenness and gluttony; we have indulged our flesh and sensual appetite; we have lived in pleasure and been wanton! We wallowed like so many swine, in the mire and dung of filthy sins, which it is a shame to speak of! We have had eyes and hearts fall of lusts and adultery, and have broken forth into such vile actual sins of immoralities, as would raise blushes in modest cheeks to hear but the mention of!

"We have been unjust and unrighteous in our dealings with others. We have wronged and defrauded our neighbor, though you have threatened to be avenged on all such people. O the *lies* we have spoken, the slanderous *backbiting* speeches that we have uttered! O the discontentment, murmuring, envying, evil desires, inordinate affections, and wicked distempers — which have been in our spirits! And though we have broken all your laws, and are guilty of such notorious sins — yet, O the impenitency and hardness of our hearts! Though no salvation is attainable but by Christ, who is freely offered unto us — yet O the unbelief of our hearts, and neglect of our own salvation! We have sinned, we have sinned against you; and what shall we do unto you, O you preserver of men!"

God expects that London should make confession of their sin, and it could be wished that London would join together like one man in this work. But if this cannot be, and they lack common mouths to open their hearts and sins before the Lord in particular confession, let every one of them be a mouth to himself, and get into his closet, and there acknowledge London's sins! And if those who are most guilty neglect this work — let God's people do it in their stead, and confess not only their own sins — but also the sins of the profane and wicked where they live, and that not only because God is dishonored — but also because they are in danger of being ruined by the unbewailed sins of others.

**5. God expects that London should be HUMBLED under these judgments.** God inflicted judgments on the children of Israel in the wilderness, "to humble them," Deuteronomy 8:16. And he promises, after the sorest distresses which he brings his people into, for their sins, to remember his covenant, "if their uncircumcised heart is humbled," Levit. 26:40-42. Yes, be promises to exalt such in due time, "who humble themselves under his mighty hand," 1 Peter 5:6.

God's mighty hand has been stretched forth upon London — he expects that London should be humble! He has humbled them by his judgments — he expects that they should humble themselves under his judgments. God has stained the pride of London — he expects that they should let down their plumes! He has brought them down — and he expects that they should lie low. God has brought poverty upon many of them in regard of their estates — and he expects that all of them should be poor in regard of their spirits. He has made many of them poor in regard of their condition — and he expects that their disposition and affection should be accordingly. God has laid many people in the dust by the *plague*, and he has laid many houses in the dust by the *fire* — and he expects that those which survive and remain after such judgments, should lay themselves in the dust for their sins!

Humble yourself then, O London, humble yourself before the Lord! Lick the dust of his feet! Put off your ornaments — and gird yourself with sackcloth, clothe yourself with humility. God has spit in your face — will you be proud of your beauty again? He has burnt the city with fire — will you be proud of your buildings and stately edifices any more? He has consumed much of the fuel of your pride — and he expects that your pride should be abated, and that you should abase yourself, and humble yourself before him!

**6. God expects that London should ACCEPT OF THE PUNISHMENT of their iniquity.** Levit. 26:40-42. "If my people shall confess their iniquity, and the iniquity of their fathers, and be humbled, and accept the punishment of their iniquity — then will I remember my covenant, and remember the land." God expects that London should *justify him* in the severest judgments which he has inflicted upon them. As they should acknowledge their sins — so they should acknowledge their demerit, and that the Lord has punished them no more — yes, that he has punished them *less* than their iniquities have deserved. As they should bring a bill of indictment against themselves — so they should bring a bill of acquittance of God.

God expects that they should say, "You are just in all that is brought upon us; for you have done right — but we have done wickedly!" Nehemiah 9:33. "O Lord, righteousness belongs unto you — but unto us confusion of faces, because we have sinned against you!" Daniel 9:7, 8.

Let not London *murmur* or *repine*, let not London find fault and complain of God, because of his judgments, Lam. 3:39. "Why does the living man complain — a man for the punishment of his sin?" God has *opened* his mouth, and spoken terribly; but let London *shut* her mouth, because God has spoken righteously! God has spoken with a loud voice — but let London be in deep silence: "I was silent, I did not open my mouth," says David, "because *you* are the one who has done this!" Psalm 39:9.

When Nadab and Abihu, the two sons of Aaron, were consumed with fire from Heaven, for offering *strange fire* before the Lord, it is said, that "Aaron was silent," Lev. 10:1-3. So when God has consumed the city of London with fire, for the sins of the inhabitants — let them be silent — because they have deserved it. Let London be silent — and know that God is righteous. Let London lay her hand upon her mouth, and her mouth in the dust! Let London close up her lips, and seal them up with silence! Or if she opens them — let her mouth be filled with confessions, not with complaints; or, if she complains — let her complain *to* God — but let her not complain *of* him. If she complains — let her complain against herself — but let her not complain against God. Let her complain of her own sin and wickedness — but not of God's judgments so righteous.

Let London be amazed that it is no worse with her — when both her *sin* and her *danger* was so great. Let her wonder, when God was so angry — that he should put any restraint upon it; that when wrath was come forth, that it proceeded no farther. Let her wonder that the plague did not quite depopulate her. Let her wonder that it is so well with her, that she is not made a desolation, and say, "It is of the Lord's mercies that we are not consumed!" Lam. 3:22.

**7. God expects that London should MOURN for her sins.** We read, "A voice was heard upon the high places, weeping and supplications of the house of Israel." Jeremiah 3:21. When the terrible voice of God's judgments has been heard in London, God hearkens for the voice of weeping and supplications — this God's voice calls for. When breaches were made in the city of David, "Then did the Lord Almighty call to weeping, and to mourning, to baldness, and to girding with sackcloth," Isaiah 22:9-11. And when instead thereof, there was "joy and gladness, eating meat, and drinking wine," the Lord is so angry, that he threatens, "surely this iniquity shall not be purged from you until you die!" verse 13, 14.

See also what the Lord calls for to the daughter of Zion under her judgments, "Let tears run down like a river day and night; give yourself no rest, let not the apple of your eye cease: arise, cry in the night; in the beginning of the watches pour out your heart like water before the face of the Lord." Lam. 2:18,19. God not only expects that "his ministers and priests should weep between the porch and the altar," when sore judgments are upon this land, as Joel 2:17; but also that the *people* should weep too, "that the bridegroom should go forth from his chamber, and the bride out of her closet," as verse 16; that people should be "afflicted, mourn and weep, that their laughter should be turned into mourning, and their joy into heaviness, James 4:9. He expects that those who escape his judgments, "should be like doves upon the mountains, every one mourning for his iniquities," as Ezekiel 6:16. London may mourn for her *judgments* which have been so dreadful — but God expects they should mourn more for *his displeasure*, which has been the cause of these judgments; and most of all for their *sins*, which have been the cause of his displeasure!

Weep London, weep for your sins, which have been so many and provoking. Let your eye affect your heart; when you look into your burying-places, and think how many of your people have lately there taken up their habitation — it should draw tears from your eyes to think of your sins, which opened the doors of those lodgings unto them! Methinks, when you pass through your ruinous habitations, and see the heaps of stones at the top of your streets, when you view your ragged walls, and open vaults, and the dismal solitude in those places, which not long ago were full of people, it should fill your heart with sorrow for your sins, which have kindled such anger in the breast of God, as to send the late dreadful fire, which has made such desolations!

Mourn, London, mourn, put on sackcloth! You see in part, what an evil and bitter thing it is to offend a holy and jealous God! The effects of sin are fearful sometimes; what evil is there in *sin*, then — which is the cause of your ruins. God expects now, that the sinners of London should become mourners. We read of a *mark* which was set upon the foreheads of those at Jerusalem, who mourned and cried out for the abominations that were done, and they were separated from temporal destruction, which was brought upon the rest, Ezekiel 9:4, 6. Just so, God sets a mark upon those who mourn in London for the sins of London; and, however, he may deal with them, in regard of temporal calamities, be sure he will separate them, and preserve them from eternal destruction.

Methinks the fall of London calls for a mourning like the mourning of Hadadrimmon in the valley of Megiddo, where Joseph fell in battle, Zech. 12:11. And there should not only be public mourning — but also private mourning, and secret mourning. It befits Christians now, after such strokes of God's wrath, to keep secret fasts, to bewail London's ruins, especially to bewail London's sins; their eyes should weep in secret places, for the abominations committed in the city, and bedew God's feet with their tears, that, if possible, they might turn away his displeasure.

God expects that London should labor to pacify his anger. When God threatened to send the sword, and to "cut off from Israel both head and tail, both palm branch and reed in a single day;" and to send the famine so sore, that "Each will feed on the flesh of his own offspring," yet it is said, "For all this his anger is not turned away — but his hand is stretched out still," Isaiah 9:14, 17, 20, 21. And now God has executed his judgments of plague and fire in London, have not we reason to fear that his anger is not yet turned away — but his hand is stretched out still?

When the houses of London were consumed, which were the fuel to the late fire, then the fire quickly went out; and if the sins of London had been consumed with the houses, if the inhabitants of the city had not brought forth their *sins*, when they were forced to leave their *goods* behind unto the flames — then we would have reason to think that the fire of God's anger was gone out, and his wrath turned away from the escaped remnant of London, insomuch as the *sins* of London have been the *fuel*, as it were, to this dreadful fire.

But when so much sin, after such judgments, is kept untouched and unmortified: when the plague of *sin* rages so much after the plague of pestilence is removed; and the fire of lust burns so much, when the other fire is extinguished: when Londoners, who have taken *new houses*, have brought into them their *old hearts,* and live in the practice of their old sins; when the swearers and profane, the drunkards and unclean, the covetous, unrighteous, and loose livers — still persevere in their wicked courses, and no judgment will put a stop to them — but they grow more hardened and incorrigible; when, as it is said, Jeremiah 5:3, the Lord has "stricken them for sin — but they are not grieved, consumed them — but they refuse to receive correction, making their faces harder than a rock, and refuse to return" — then what can we conclude — but that God's anger still remains, yes, is more enraged by this aggravation of their wickedness, and that he is stretching forth his hand to give them another blow!

God expects that London should use some means to pacify his anger, and he gives them time for it by the *pauses* which he makes between his judgments, being still slow to anger, and unwilling, if he is not even forced unto it, utterly to destroy this place, where his name has been called upon. O that London would be persuaded upon this duty, which so much concerns their safety and happiness!

When the fire was in London, and it burned so furiously and dreadfully on the Monday and Tuesday, Londoners' hearts were sunk within them, having little hopes of getting victory over this conqueror, which marched through their streets; and therefore little resistance was made — but all were busily employed in flying from him, with their goods. But when the fury of the fire was somewhat abated on the Wednesday, and they began to conceive any hopes that it might be extinguished, then they pluck up their spirits, and join their forces, and many thousand hands are at work in drawing water, and pouring them upon the flames, and their pains, through God's blessing, was not unsuccessful.

The *fire of God's wrath*, which shall devour the wicked, and burn them everlastingly, will be so furious and dreadful, that the hearts of the damned will sink under it without the least hope of ever extinguishing this flame, or flying from it, when it has once got hold of them; and therefore they will not attempt — but let alone all endeavors forever to turn away God's displeasure, and to put out the unquenchable fire of Hell.

But the fire of God's wrath and anger *now* may be put out, and the flames of his *anger* — may be turned into flames of *love*. God's *anger*, which has been so hot against London, may be cooled; his *wrath* may be alleviated, and his displeasure removed. There is hope concerning this thing. God is not yet grown so furious that he will not be spoken unto; he is easy to be entreated, and therefore London may be encouraged in their endeavors to pacify his anger. Let them not say, as Israel of old, Jeremiah 2:25, "There is no hope; no, for I have loved strangers, and after them will I go." Though God's anger is not yet turned away — yet it *may* be turned away; and though *one hand* be stretched out to destroy you — yet the other hand is stretched forth to save you; "for he stretches forth his hand all the day long, to a disobedient and obstinate people," Romans 10:21.

O labor then to pacify God's anger — to quench this fire! Arise and gird yourselves with humility; pluck up your spirits, and stir up yourselves to lay hold on God, and stop him in the march of his judgments! Bring forth your buckets, draw water, and pour it forth before the Lord; let your eyes be like fountains of tears; the voice of weeping, and mourning for sin — turns God's affections within him, Jeremiah 31:18-20. "I have surely heard Ephraim bemoaning himself, 'You disciplined me like an unruly calf, and I have been disciplined. Restore me, and I will return, because you are the Lord my God. After I strayed, I repented; after I came to understand, I beat my breast. I was ashamed and humiliated because I bore the disgrace of my youth.'" And when he repented after such chastisements, and was ashamed of his sin — God relents, and his affections are moved for him: "Is not Ephraim my dear son, the child in whom I delight? Though I often speak against him, I still remember him. Therefore my heart yearns for him; I have great compassion for him, says the Lord."

If London would be chastised, and receive the impressions of grief and shame for their sins by these judgments, God's affections would be moved, and his fierce anger would be changed into tender compassion; and though he has spoken *terribly* against London — yet he would now speak *comfortably* unto her; he would earnestly remember her, and make her glad according to the days wherein he has afflicted her, and the years wherein she has seen evil. There is an excellent virtue in the *tears of true repentance*, accompanied with the *blood of Christ*, applied by *faith* — to quench the fire of God's anger!

"God is angry with the wicked every day!" Psalm 7:11. Lost sinners, God is angry with you! It is worse to have God angry with you — than all the men in the world! His favor is better than life — his displeasure is worse than death!

To have God angry with you, who is so just and jealous, who is so potent and furious — is very dreadful. If the wrath of an earthly king is like the roaring of a lion — then what is the wrath of the King of Heaven? And when His anger is stirred up by your sins, and blown into a flame, and breaks forth upon you — what will you do?

You cannot hide yourselves in any place where His all-seeing eye will not find you! You cannot fly into any place where His stretched-forth arm will not reach you! You cannot gather such strength as to defend yourselves from the strokes of his vengeance! "Who can stand in His sight when once He is angry?" Psalm 86:7

O then labor to pacify His anger! You cannot fly *from* Him — O then, fly *unto* Him!

You cannot stand in His sight when he is angry — O then, fall down at His feet, make peace with this omnipotent adversary, while you are upon the way, before He delivers you to the officer, 'death' — and casts you into the prison of Hell!

Lost sinners, God's *patience* does as yet hold his *arm!* His mercy calls upon you to repent, and he invites you to make your peace with him, Isaiah 27:4, 5; "Who would set the briers and thorns against me in battle? I would go through them, I would burn them together! Let them come to me for refuge; let them make peace with me, yes, let them make peace with me." You will be like briers and thorns, which will easily take fire, and quickly be consumed in the time of God's anger; and if briers and thorns offer to contend with devouring fire, what will be the outcome — but the burning them up without remedy?

You will find it sharp and painful for your feet — if you kick against the goads; you will dash out your brains — if you run your head against a rock, or a bronze wall. Just so, none ever hardened themselves against God, and prospered; none ever fought against the God of Heaven by their sins — but they were wounded, and in the end destroyed!

Sin, when it is finished — brings forth death, and wrath, and misery forever! O then, lay hold on God's strength, and make peace with him! Run to him, take hold of the *scepter of grace* and reconciliation, which is held forth unto you! Take hold of his *arm*, and plead with him for mercy! Take hold of his *Son*, who is offered to you, who is set forth to be an atoning sacrifice for the remission of sins, through the forbearance of God, Romans 3:25. As yet God has forborne you; as yet you are on this side of the grave and Hell; and there is a possibility of turning away God's anger, which is kindled against you, of flying from that wrath which is pursuing of you, of escaping those miseries which are preparing for you — and therefore lay hold on Christ who is freely offered unto you, who is able and willing to save you, and make your peace with the Father, and to procure a pardon for you.

And further to move you, you are not only offered peace and reconciliation — but you are *entreated* to be reconciled; ministers entreat you; yes, God himself, and Jesus Christ by us, entreats, and prays, and beseeches you — that you would accept of reconciliation, 2 Corinthians 5:20. Be astonished, O you Heavens, and wonder, O angels! Be astonished much more, O you sinners, and be enrapt up with admiration, O you rebels! The King of glory, against whom you have rebelled, and who could crush you so easily without any injury to himself, is not only *willing* to lay aside his anger — but also *entreats* you to accept of reconciliation!

Heartily embrace Jesus Christ upon his own terms, and the work will be done! Otherwise the fury of the Lord will be so much the more provoked, and the fire of his anger will break forth into such a flame, as none shall be able to quench! Otherwise the Lord will be so much the more *enraged* against you, and meet you like a roaring and devouring lion, or like a bear bereaved of her whelps — and rend your heart, yes, tear you in pieces, when there shall be none to deliver you!

**9. God expects that London should TURN from her evil ways!** The Lord makes a sweet promise under the dreadful judgments of famine or pestilence, which sometimes he sends upon his people for their sins: "If my people, which are called by name, shall humble themselves, and pray, and seek my face, and turn from their wicked ways — then will I hear from Heaven, and forgive their sins, and will heal their land." 2 Chron. 7:14.

God not only expects that Londoners should now *acknowledge* their sins, and *humble* themselves, and *mourn* for their sins; but also that they should ***turn*** from them — otherwise pardon, and healing, and his favor, is not to be obtained, neither are further judgments likely to be prevented. They must "confess and *forsake* their sins — if they would find mercy." Proverbs 28:13. "The wicked must *forsake* their way of sin, and *turn* unto the Lord — and *then* he will have mercy, and abundantly pardon," Isaiah 55:7. God threatens to go on to punish such as go on to transgress; Psalm 68:21, "God will smash the heads of his enemies, crushing the skulls of those who love their guilty ways."

Break off, then, your sins by repentance, and cast away all your transgressions from you; put away the evil of your doings, from before the holy and jealous eyes of God; cease to do evil, cleanse your hands, you sinners, and purify your hearts, you wickedly-minded; wash yourselves in the fountain of Christ's blood, set open to you, that you may be cleansed from all filthiness of flesh and spirit — and be partakers of holiness, and the divine nature. Deny all ungodliness and worldly lusts; abstain from flesh-pleasing sins, which war against the soul; and be not conformed to the wicked customs of wicked men! Neither follow this ungodly generation to do evil; much less run with them to the same excess of riot — but be transformed by the renewing of your minds, and live soberly, righteously, and godly in this present evil world! Let the time past of your lives, be sufficient wherein you have wrought the will of the flesh, and served divers lusts, and cast a blot upon the profession of Christianity; now be blameless, and harmless, and unrebukable in the midst of a crooked and perverse nation. Cast off the works of darkness; lay aside your night-veil of ignorance; put on the robes of light; walk honestly, as in the day, shining as lights where you live. Forbear all works of darkness and sin; and as the One who called you is holy — you also are to be holy in all your conduct.

Sinners, turn from your evil ways, otherwise your iniquity will be your eternal ruin.

**1. DRUNKARDS**, turn from your evil ways! "Do not gaze at wine when it is red, when it sparkles in the cup, when it goes down smoothly! In the end it bites like a snake and poisons like a viper!" Proverbs 23:31-32. Wounds and woe are the outcome of excessive drinking, verse 29. This sin may be sweet and pleasing to the eye and appetite in the temptation — but it will wound and sting the conscience, worse than an adder or serpent can do the body, in the reflection!

God has put bitterness into the cup by his judgments — and will you drink as deep as before? Are you resolved to taste the *dregs* which lie at the bottom? The cup has *poison* in it — foul poison, and will you drink of it still, though you murder and destroy your souls forever by this sin! The cup has *wrath* in it — the wrath of an angry God! Is it good for you to drink of the wine of God's wrath? Drunkenness has been your sin, and if you go on, God threatens that drunkenness shall be your punishment, Jeremiah 13:12, "This is what the Lord, the God of Israel, says: Every wineskin should be filled with wine." Drunkards like this very well; they are very well pleased that their bottles shall be filled with wine, that they may empty them; but understand the meaning, verse 13, 14. "Thus says the Lord, I will fill all the inhabitants of the land with drunkenness; and I will smash them one against the other, fathers and sons alike, declares the Lord. I will allow no pity or mercy or compassion to keep me from destroying them!"

Drunkards, you reel and fall sometimes with your sin: God will make you reel and fall by his judgments, and dash you one upon another; yes, dash you in pieces, and destroy you without pity or mercy! Will you not then, forbear your cups and excesses? God will put a cup of trembling and astonishment into your hand; he will put gall and wormwood into your cup, and make you taste the bitter effects of this sin! If he does not severely scourge you for this sin here — he will be sure to torment you for this sin forever!

Turn, you drunkards, from your evil ways! *Vomit up your sin* by repentance! Weep and mourn for all your sinful mirth and jollity! And take heed of returning with the dog, and licking up the vomit which you have disgorged.

Avoid all occasions of this sin — shun the company of such as have been your tempters — take heed of coming into the places where you have been drawn in to commit it. Make a covenant with your feet, that they may never lead you out of the way of God, into such places, where you have been so often overtaken. Curb and restrain your *appetite*; take some kind of *holy revenge* upon yourselves; deny yourselves some things which are lawful in themselves, if they are *occasions of sin* unto you. Instead of filling yourselves with wine, or strong drink unto drunkenness and excess — labor to be filled with the Spirit, and by the Spirit to mortify this and all other deeds of the body. Let the wicked wonder at you, and speak evil of you for your sobriety — rather than God hate you, and bring destruction upon you for your intemperance!

**2. ADULTERERS**, turn from your evil ways! Come out of the unclean bed! Do not wallow any longer in this besmearing mire! Have you fallen into the *filthy ditch*? Get up and come forth with speed, and wash your garments from the spots, which they have received. Are you taken in the *net*, and ensnared in adulterous embracements? Deliver yourselves like a deer from the net of the hunter, and like a bird from the snare of the fowler.

Do not lust after the beauty and enjoyment of adulterous women; do nor let the soft and sweet language of their lips entice you, nor the sparkling motions of their eyes inflame you! Do not put *fire* into your bosoms, and take heed of walking upon burning coals! Why will you consume your body, and time, and substance, which cannot be regained? Why will you bring upon yourselves a wound and dishonor — which cannot be wiped off. Why will you be like *oxen* which go to the slaughter — and be such *fools* as to bring upon yourselves eternal destruction?

Turn from your evil ways! Do not dare to go forward in that way which leads unto death and Hell. "God will judge the adulterer and all the sexually immoral!" Hebrews 13:4. God has shot his arrows into the city, and wounded many adulterers for this sin, who had before defiled and wounded themselves by it! And will you go on, until a dart pierces through your liver? The *beginning* of the sin is sweet, like honey — but will not the *end* be more bitter than wormwood? And if a *little short pleasure of the flesh* is so desirable — will not the *extreme endless pain* it will produce be intolerable? Can you be content to lie so many millions of years, under the horrible tortures of Hell, for a little present sensual delight, which, when reaped, cannot yield you satisfaction! Is it sweet to fall into the arms of an adulterous woman? And will it not be a bitter and "a fearful thing to fall into the hands of the living God?" Hebrews 10:31 — especially when he is irreconcilably angry, and his anger burns like fire which is devouring, and unquenchable?

You have seen the fire which has burnt down the city — how dreadful it was! The *fire of lust* within you is worse; and the *fire of Hell* beneath you, which is preparing for you, and unto which, by this sin, you are hastening — is a thousand fold more dreadful! And yet will you go on? O turn from your adulterous ways; do not come near the doors of such houses, where you have had incentives to lust, and opportunities for such lewd practices! Make a covenant with your *eyes* — the *spark* is caught at the eye — the spark that, falling upon the *tinder of an adulterous heart* — puts it into a flame!

Do not *look* upon the maiden — that you may not *think!*

Do not *think* — that you may not *lust.*

Do not *touch* — that you may not desire to *taste.*

Do not *toy* — lest you be *caught!*

Do not come *near the brink* — lest you fall into the stream before you are aware!

If you would be kept from *actual* immorality — take heed of *mental* immorality! Take heed of *self-pollutions* — as you would be kept from adultery with *others!* Avoid occasions of this sin, do not come into such company and places where you may have opportunity to commit it! *Flee* youthful lusts which war against the soul! Keep your minds pure and chaste! Resist the *first suggestions* to this sin — quench the fire when it begins to kindle! Look to the *outcome* and *consequences* of this sin! Above all, remember that the holy eye of God is upon you, in your most secret retirements, and he will, before long, call you to an account!

**3. SWEARERS**, turn from your evil ways. Remember the third commandment, unto which a threatening is annexed, "You shall not take the name of the Lord your God in vain — for the Lord will not hold him guiltless, who takes his name in vain." Exodus 20:7. The very use of the name of God *irreverently*, is a breach of this command. But to *swear* by the name of God, in ordinary discourse, is a gross breach of it; which, as it affronts God highly, so it will bring condemnation certainly upon the guilty, who do not repent and forbear.

When God has made your mouths, and given you tongues to speak his praise, which then are your glory — will you profane the name of this God, and turn not only the glory of God — but also your own glory, into shame and dishonor — and that, when you have not the motive and incentive to flesh-pleasing sins?

Look into Deuteronomy 28:58, 59, what threatenings the Lord denounces here against such as do not *fear* his name! And surely it is for lack of fear and awe of God's name, that any are so bold as to swear by it, or take it in vain: "If you do not carefully follow all the words of this law, which are written in this book, and do not *revere this glorious and awesome name* — the Lord your God — the Lord will send fearful plagues on you and your descendants, harsh and prolonged *disasters*, and severe and lingering illnesses."

Has not God plagued and burned the city of London, among other sins, for this of *swearing* — and yet will you swear still, and provoke the Lord to further wrath — when you have seen, in part, how fearful the name of God is, in the judgments which he has executed! Will you go on *still* to profane his name? Do you not fear future judgments? Will not the name of God be displayed more dreadfully before you, when he opens the *treasury of his wrath*, and sends his Son in flaming fire to take vengeance upon sinners? And yet will not you fear this holy name of God?

Swearers, with what confidence can you *pray* to God? What hope can you have, when you use God's name in prayer, that you shall have the least audience or acceptance — when you abuse his name so much, and cast such dishonor upon it, by your oaths? If you do not pray now, as swearers seldom do — will you never be driven to your knees — when no creature shall be able to give you any relief? And with what face can you, then, look up to God? Will not your callings upon the name of God be in vain — as you have taken his name in vain? Will not God laugh at your calamity? And though you cry and shout, will not he shut out your prayer, and bar the *door of mercy* upon you forever?

Swearers, turn from your sin! Make a covenant with your mouth! Set a watch before the door of your lips! Use God's name in prayer, and *reverently* in discourse. Do not swear by it, or take it in vain anymore; get an *awe* of this name upon your hearts, which will be an excellent means to keep you from this sin.

**4. LIARS**, turn from your evil ways. We read Acts 5, of Ananias and Sapphira, who were smitten with sudden death for the sin of lying. It is said, "they fell down at the apostles' feet, and died." And has not the sin of lying been one ingredient in the meritorious cause of the fall of so many people and houses by the *plague* and *fire* in the city of London?

This sin of lying, the apostle especially cautions the Colossians and Ephesians against, after the wonderful grace of God in the renovation of them according to his image, Colossians 3:9, "Do not lie, one to another, seeing you have put off the old man, with his deeds, and have put on the new man," etc. Ephesians 4:24,

25. "Having put on the new man, which, after God is created in righteousness and true holiness. Put away lying, and speak every man truth to his neighbor."

And this sin, I may caution Londoners against, after the dreadful anger of God expressed in the desolations which he has made among them by his late judgments. Do not lie to one another any more — but speak every one, truth to his neighbor. The *Lord* is a God of truth — and he cannot lie. The *devil* is the father of lies and liars, John 8:44. Which is most desirable — to be children of God, or children of the devil?

A lying tongue is one of the seven abominations which the Lord hates, Proverbs 6:16,17. And is there any *good* you can get by your lying, comparable to the *evil* of rendering yourselves hateful and abominable in the sight of God? Is it *needful* for you sometimes to speak lies? Is it not a thousand-fold more needful for you always to speak truth? Are you likely to gain so much by lying — as by telling the truth? What is a little outward gain — in comparison with inward peace? What is the loss of external, temporal things — in comparison with the loss of your souls and happiness forever? Is it needful to lie — that you may excuse your faults? This makes them doubly heinous!

Parents, warn your *children* against this sin of lying; do not spare the *rod of correction* where you find them guilty; pass by twenty other faults rather than this. Lying is the first link in the chain of a thousand gross sins! Knock off their fingers from the *first link* — lest the chain afterwards grows too strong for you to break.

Masters, indulge not your servants in this sin; the resolution of David was, Psalm 101:7, "No one who practices *deceit* will dwell in my house; no one who speaks *falsely* will stand in my presence!" Especially take heed of leading servants to this sin by your example! Above all, of putting them upon this sin, by your persuasions or commands; for, besides the guilt of their sin, which hereby you incur, your damage is likely to be more than your advantage by their lies. If you put them upon lying *for* you, they will put themselves upon lying *to* you; and if you deceive others in some things by the former, they are likely to deceive you, deservedly, in greater things by the latter.

*Young ones*, take heed of lies! Do nothing which may need the *cloak* and *excuse* of a lie! And if you are overtaken with a fault — never *deny* it; but with sorrow acknowledge it, as you would gain favor with God and man. Take heed of this sin *early* — lay aside lying before it grows into a *habit*, which will be hard to leave.

*Old ones*, break off this sin, before you be *dragged by the chain of this sin into the fire of Hell*, which is the threatened punishment thereof, Rev. 21:8. "But the cowardly, the unbelieving, the vile, the murderers, the sexually immoral, those who practice magic arts, the idolaters and all **liars** — their place will be in the fiery lake of burning sulfur!" Revelation 21:8. Be not too *hasty in speech*, lest this sin issue forth at the *door of your lips*, before you are aware! Speak always as in the *hearing of God*, who knows whether your *word* and *heart* agree, and who will one day call you to an account for this sin; and, except you repent, punish you for it severely in the lake of fire and brimstone!

**5. SLANDERERS**, turn from your evil ways. The sin of slandering is one of the worst sorts of lying, and the teeth of slanderers are compared to "spears and arrows, and their tongues to a sharp sword!" Psalm 57:4; and when they utter their slanders, they "bend their bow, and shoot their arrows, they whet their sword!" And they wound therewith, the reputation of others, which they are bound to be as careful of, as their own.

Slanderers are "false witnesses, who lay to the charge of others, such things as they know not," Psalm 35:11. They are *lions* — who tear in pieces the good name of others! They are *serpents* — whose words are stings, and full of deadly poison! They are compared to "clubs, and swords, and sharp arrows," Proverbs 25:18. Yes, they are like "mad men, who cast about firebrands, and arrows, and death!" Proverbs 26:18.

By this sin, you wound others, and are guilty of *tongue*-murder! But you wound yourselves more — I mean your consciences, and are guilty of self-murder, of soul-murder! The poison of such speeches is not so venomous and deadly, in regard of your neighbor's good name — as it is in regard of your own spirits, which are envenomed, and will be destroyed hereby — without the application of the blood of Christ for pardon and healing!

Slanderers, forbear your backbiting, slanderous speeches! Forbear devouring words, which swallow up the good name of your neighbors! Do not let your throats be like *open sepulchers* — to entomb their reputation. Take heed that your tongues do not utter slanders and reproaches, devised by yourselves; be careful also that you do not *spread* such calumnies as *others* have devised. Do not receive any accusation against your neighbors, without good proof! Drive away backbiting tongues — with an angry countenance! And if you must hear of other faults, let *love conceal* them as much as may be from the knowledge of others; rather speak what you bear to *themselves*, and reprove them (if the things are scandalous) with prudence, love, and a spirit of meekness.

Remember the command, Titus 3:2, "Speak evil of no man." And take heed of the sinful practice of the women described, 1 Tim. 5:13. "They get into the habit of being idle and going about from house to house. And not only do they become idlers, but also *gossips* and *busybodies*, saying things they ought not to."

Where your tongues have been instrumental to wound others, and yourselves withal, by slanderous speeches — now make use of the same instrument, for healing. Labor to heal yourselves by confession of your sins to God — and to heal others by acknowledging to them the wrong you have done them. Labor by good words, to promote their esteem, which you have unjustly taken away. Labor for so much humility and brotherly love, as to be as tender of their good name and fame — as of your own; and in honor to prefer them above yourselves, which will make you ready to *hide their faults*, and keep you from *evil surmises* and evil slanderous speeches!

**6. REVILERS**, turn from your evil ways! *Reviling* and *slandering* often go together — as proceeding both from the same *root* of malice and hatred; yet, sometimes, the sin of **malice** is kept more secret. When war is in the heart, and mischief is inwardly devised, and the name secretly wounded with slanders behind the back — then the *tongue flatters*, and like a honey-comb, drops nothing but sweet words before the face of the slandered one! But the sin of **reviling** is open, and spits forth rancour and malice into the face, and breaks forth into bitter speeches, for the shame and disgrace of such people against whom they are spoken — though revilers disgrace themselves more, by the weakness, and poor government of spirit, which hereby they reveal.

Revilers, refrain your angry bitter speeches; "Let all bitterness, and wrath, and anger, and clamor, and evil speaking, be put away from you, with all malice!" Ephesians 4. Do not quarrel and contend: do not break forth into brawls and clamors, and bitter reviling speeches, against such as give you no occasion — but desire to live at peace with you. And if others are angry, and quarrel with you — then labor to pacify their anger; do not *stir up the coals* by your bitter retorts, "Do not repay evil with evil or insult with insult, but with blessing, because to this you were called so that you may inherit a blessing!" 1 Peter 3:9.

Like our Savior, "When they hurled their insults at him, he did not retaliate; when he suffered, he made no threats. Instead, he entrusted himself to him who judges justly." 1 Peter 2:23.

The *second blow* breeds the quarrel, and the *second reviling word* breeds the strife! Give to a hard speech — the return of a soft answer. Proverbs 15:1. "A gentle answer turns away anger — but a harsh word stirs up wrath." And Proverbs 25:15. "A ruler can be persuaded through patience, and a gentle tongue can break a bone."

There is a *marvelous force* in a meek reception of bitter speeches — to appease anger, and mollify the spirits of those which are most fierce. Whereas grievous and bitter replies, stir up unto greater contention. Do not take revenge with the *hand* — neither take revenge with the *tongue*! Do not revile enemies — but "love them, and pray for them, and do good to them; feed and clothe them," Matthew 5:44; Romans 12:19, 20. "Be gentle, showing all meekness to all men," Titus 3:2.

Especially, do not revile your friends! Take heed of stirring up strife in the house where you live; be of a peaceable disposition. Above all, take heed of reviling *Christ's* friends, God's children — do not revile the saints. Remember that no revilers, especially such revilers as persevere in that sin, who "shall inherit the kingdom of God!" 1 Corinthians 6:10. And when the Lord Jesus comes at the last day, He will execute judgment upon the ungodly, for their "hard speeches which they have spoken against him, in speaking against his people," Jude 15.

Revilers, govern your tongues! "If any man among you seems to be religious, and bridles not his tongue — that man's religion is vain!" Would you govern yourselves well, according to scripture rules — and bridle and govern your tongues? "Now when we put bridles into the mouths of horses to make them obey us, we also guide the whole animal. And consider ships: Though very large and driven by fierce winds, they are guided by a very small rudder wherever the will of the pilot directs." James 3:3-4. Put a *bridle* upon this little member, and you may the better have all the rest at command, and keep yourselves under control, when otherwise vented passions, like wild horses without reins, otherwise the fierce storms of your minds may break forth, and drive you upon rocks and shelves, and shipwreck both soul and body together!

"Likewise the *tongue* is a small part of the body, but it makes great boasts. Consider what a great forest is set on fire by a small spark. The tongue also is a fire, a world of evil among the parts of the body. It corrupts the whole person, sets the whole course of his life on fire, and is itself set on fire by hell!" James 3:5-6. Get the former fire quenched — get the heat of your tongues cooled; as you would escape the latter fire — I mean the fire of Hell, from whence the former fire proceeds, and unto which it will certainly bring you!

"All kinds of animals, birds, reptiles and creatures of the sea are being tamed and have been *tamed* by man — but no man can tame the tongue. It is a restless evil, full of deadly poison!" James 3:7-8. You cannot tame your tongues — but you may get them tamed: put them under the *government of Christ* — and *he* will tame them! Get your passions tamed within, and you may tame this deadly member! Keep guard and sentinel before the *door of your lips*, and watch your words — that you offend not with your tongues.

**7. PERSECUTORS**, turn from your evil ways. Forbear persecuting the people of God, who desire your good, and are the best safeguard and defense, by their prayers and faith, of the places where they live, from miseries and destruction. Is it good for you to *saw on the bough* on which you stand over such a deep chasm, into which, if you would fall, it will be impossible for you to recover yourselves again? Is it good for you to *pull at the pillars* of the house, which, if you pluck down, will bring the house upon you, and bury you in its ruins? Is it good to put yourselves under the heavy millstone which will grind you to powder?

Suppose, while you are breathing forth threatenings against any of Christ's disciples, and are in the heat of your rage and furious persecution of them — that you should hear such a voice as Paul did from Heaven, "Sinners, sinners, why are you persecuting me?" Would it not hinder, and stop you? You may hear this voice, if you will open your ear unto the Word — it is Christ you *persecute* in his disciples; it is Christ you *wound* through their sides; you would do the same to him as the Jews did, were he alive among you, and you had the same power as was put into their hands against the Lord of Life.

I will not charge London with, and therefore need not warn them generally against, the sin of persecution of God's people — because they have been a shelter to them, when the times have frowned most upon them; but are there none who have need of this warning? Are there no *Judas's* among them, none of Paul's persecuting spirit before his conversion?

Persecutors, forbear this sin, which makes you as much like the devil as any that I know — and locks you fastest in his arms; which is the very next door to the sin against the Holy Spirit; which will bring upon you swift destruction; which will sink you into the lower parts of the bottomless pit; which will lash and sting your consciences with horrible scourges hereafter — if they be not awakened with horror here! Turn from this sin before it is too late; imitate Paul, and become friends to them, against whom you have expressed so much enmity and spite.

**8. COVETOUS** people, turn from your evil ways! God has smitten you for the iniquity of your covetousness — do not go frowardly on in this sin! He has subtracted much of the *fuel* of this sin, and burnt it in the fire — let there be a greater decay in your lust of covetousness, than there has been in any of your estates. Covetousness is one of the sins which the apostles would not have "so much as named among the saints," Ephesians 5:3. It is a sin if it reigns. It is inconsistent with the truth of grace, and power of godliness, because it is idolatry! Colossians 3:5. And the apostle tells us expressly, that "covetous people shall not inherit the kingdom of God," 1 Corinthians 9:10. Yes, that "the wrath of God shall come upon them!" Ephesians 5:6.

Covetous people, turn from your sin — get your *hearts* loosened from those things, which you have hitherto made your God, and in which you have sought for your chief felicity.

Have you *little* in the world? Be *contented* with the portion which God gives you — you have as much as God sees fit for you! Hebrews 13:5. "Keep your lives free from the love of money and *be content with what you have.*" Covetousness will not heal your poverty, any more than riches can heal your covetousness.

Have you *much* in the world? Do your riches increase? Do not set your heart upon them. Make use of what God has given you without such pinching and self-denial, which the Lord Jesus never commanded in his precepts of that kind. God never gave riches to *save* — but to *use.* Do not spare the moderate use of what you have, for fear of future lack; use part of your estates for yourselves in what is needful for the body, and suitable to your degree and quality; lay *aside* part for your posterity; and lay *out* part in the help of those in necessity, for relief of the poor, whereby "you will lay up for yourselves a good foundation for the time to come; and, at last, lay hold on eternal life!" 1 Tim. 6:18, 19.

**9. UNRIGHTEOUS** people, turn from your evil ways! God has been righteous in his judgments — because you have been unrighteous in your dealings! And as his judgments are a reproof of your sin — so are they a warning to you to leave it. Unrighteous gains will yield you little advantage in the outcome. See what the Apostle James speaks of the wealth which men get in such a way,

"Now listen, you rich people, weep and wail because of the misery that is coming upon you. Your wealth has rotted, and moths have eaten your clothes. Your gold and silver are corroded. Their corrosion will testify against you and eat your flesh like fire. You have hoarded wealth in the last days. Look! The wages you failed to pay the workmen who mowed your fields are crying out against you. The cries of the harvesters have reached the ears of the Lord Almighty. You have lived on earth in luxury and self-indulgence. You have fattened yourselves in the day of slaughter!" James 5:1-5

The *curse of God* goes along with unlawful, unrighteous gains; and is like *moth* and *rust* to *corrupt* and *canker* them; they bring a fire into the flesh and bones, which will eat and torment; they pierce men through with many sorrows, and at the latter end utterly consume them with terrors, if their conscience becomes awakened. Unrighteous people do not heap up such *treasures of wealth* — as by sin they heap up a *treasury of wrath* against themselves in the last day. The wrongs which they do to others, cry with a loud voice to God; and the Lord will be the avenger of all such as are defrauded. Let those who have been unrighteous — then be unrighteous no more!

You cannot wrong others so much by this sin — as you wrong yourselves! Shake your hands of dishonest gains; make restitution of what you have defrauded others, as you expect salvation. This is a hard saying to some, who have no other wealth but what they have gained in a dishonest and unrighteous way; but will it not be harder to suffer *the vengeance of eternal fire* for this sin? Is it not better to impoverish yourselves, that you may be just and honest while you live — than to be damned and thrust into a place of eternal torment when you die?

You must soon leave all that you have; and if God does not take away what you have by some temporal calamity before — be sure that *death* will strip you of all! And is it not better for you to part with it yourselves to the just owners, when this is the way to obtain pardon and peace, and an eternal inheritance, which is of a thousand-fold more value? And do not fear that God will make no provision for you while you abide in the world, if you resolve to be honest, and put your trust in him, who has the disposal of the earth and the fullness thereof. Be righteous for the future; do not swerve a hair from the *rule of right*. "So in everything, do to others what you would have them do to you;" this is a principle inscribed upon the heart by nature, "for this sums up the Law and the Prophets," Matthew 7:12.

**10. HYPOCRITES**, turn you from your evil ways! Methinks the terrible voice of God should affrighten you, under your hypocritical shows, and external devotions! Methinks you should now bend your *hearts* to please the Lord, and approve yourselves chiefly to him, who has expressed so much displeasure against sinners, and is most highly offended with *hypocrites*. What good will a *mere form* do for you — without the power of godliness? What good will *religious shows* do you — without sincere and substantial service? What benefit will you get by counterfeit graces? If your repentance, and faith, and love, and the like, are only pretended — how ineffectual will they be to procure eternal pardon, and peace, and salvation? Are you content to lose all your external religion, and to have all your heartless lifeless duties rise up one day in judgment against you?

What advantage will you get by a bare profession of religion, especially in such times when profession, if it is strict, is discountenanced; and professors, if their lamp shines with any brightness, and they carry any great sail, expose themselves to danger? And if you have not *heart-sincerity*, which alone can yield you the true and sweet fruits of true religion — you are likely to lose all, and of all others to make yourselves most miserable. You may suffer from *men* — because you have a profession; and you will suffer from *God* — because you have no more than a profession! What then, should you cast off your profession? If so, you would turn apostates, and may fall into the sin against the Holy Spirit, which will bring upon you inevitable damnation. But lay aside your hypocrisy, and become sincere. Be that in truth — which you are in show; labor for *sincerity* in regard of your state, and in regard of your duties.

Lost sinners, God calls upon all of you to turn from your evil ways by his thundering voice.

Turn *now!* Let the time past, be sufficient wherein you have fulfilled the desires of the flesh and the mind; do not go a step forward in the way of sin, lest you meet with destruction suddenly, and perish without remedy!

Turn *universally*. Do not say of any sin, as Lot did of Zoar, "It is a *little* one!" Cast away *all* your transgressions, and let *no iniquity* have dominion over you for the future.

Turn *heartily*, from an inward principle of hatred to sin, and love to God; and not from external considerations, and merely upon the account of sin's dreadful consequences.

Turn *continually*, and with full purpose of heart, never to return unto your evil ways of sin any more.

**10. By the fire which burnt down the city — the Lord expects that London should SEEK him**; that they should not only *turn* from their evil ways — but also that they should "turn unto him who has smitten them, and seek the Lord almighty," Isaiah 9:13. We read in Amos 5:2. "The virgin of Israel is fallen, she is forsaken — and none to raise her up!" Whereupon God calls this duty, verse 4-8. "Thus says the Lord to the house of Israel, Seek me — and you shall live; but seek not Bethel, etc. Seek the Lord, and you shall live, lest he break forth like fire and devour, and there be none to quench; seek him who made the seven stars, and Orion, and turns the shadow of death into the morning, etc. The Lord is his name!" And it follows, verse 15. "It may be, that the Lord will be gracious unto the remnant of Joseph." And when this duty is neglected, see the *threatening*, verse 16. "Wailing shall be in all streets, and they shall say in all the highways: Alas, alas! and they shall call the farmers to mourning, and such as are skillful of lamentation, to wailing."

And now London is fallen, does not the Lord call upon them — that they would call upon him? And as they would turn away his anger, and prevent their utter ruin — that they would seek him who can turn the *shadow of death* — into the morning, and the *blackest night of affliction* — into a day of prosperity and rejoicing.

London, seek the Lord, that you may live, that there may be a reviving after the years of such death and ruins! Seek the Lord, before the decree brings forth some other judgment, and you pass away like chaff before the whirlwind, in the day of the Lord's fierce anger. It may be the Lord will be gracious to the remnant of this great city.

God expects that London should now *pray* at another rate than heretofore they have done. It is said, Dan. 9:13. "All this disaster has come upon us — yet we have not sought the favor of the Lord our God by turning from our sins and giving attention to your truth!" And when God had consumed Israel, because of their iniquities, the prophet complains, Isaiah 45:7. "There is none who calls upon your name, who stirs up himself to take hold of you!" Had the prayers of London been such as they should have been — the desolations of London might have been prevented! God expects that London, under such chastisements should "pour out prayers before him," Isaiah 26:16.

God has *spoken terribly* unto them, he expects that they should *cry mightily* unto him. God expects that London should meet him in the way of his judgments, not only with *weepings for their sins*, that they have provoked him unto so great displeasure — but also with *supplications for his mercies*. When Jacob was devoured, and his dwelling-place laid waste — you have their prayer, "Do not hold against us the sins of the fathers; may your mercy come quickly to meet us, for we are in desperate need. Help us, O God our Savior, for the glory of your name; deliver us and forgive our sins for your name's sake!" Psalms 79:8-9

And the church, under desolating judgments, does in prayer express herself very pathetically, "Look down from heaven and see from your lofty throne, holy and glorious. Where are your zeal and your might? Your tenderness and compassion are withheld from us. But you O Lord, are our Father, our Redeemer from of old is your name!" Isaiah 63:15-16. "Yet, O Lord, you are our Father. We are the clay, you are the potter; we are all the work of your hand. Do not be angry beyond measure, O Lord; do not remember our sins forever. Oh, look upon us, we pray, for we are all your people!" Isaiah 64:8-9

God has been pleading and contending with London by his judgments — and God looks that London should plead with him in prayer for his mercies.

London, seek the Lord Almighty, who has come forth against you in battle, and wounded you with his sharp arrows, and as yet has not laid down his weapons! Get to your knees; hang about God's feet and arms; fill your mouths with arguments to halt him in the course of his judgments. Do not let your eye cease from weeping, that you have displeased him; and do not let your tongue cease from humble and earnest entreaties, that he would pardon you, and remove his displeasure from you.

Seek the Lord *humbly* — put your mouths in the dust, if so be there may be any hope. God hears the cry of the humble, and will not despise their prayer, Psalm 10:17; Psalm 102:17.

Seek the Lord *diligently* — he has promised to be found by all those who *diligently* seek him. God looks for earnest, hearty, fervent prayer. There is a sweet promise which God makes to his people's prayers after his sore judgments which he had brought upon them, "For I know the plans I have for you," declares the Lord, "plans to prosper you and not to harm you, plans to give you hope and a future. Then you will call upon me and come and pray to me, and I will listen to you. You will seek me and find me when you seek me with all your heart." Jeremiah 29:11-13

Seek the Lord *believingly* — mingle your prayers with faith, and make use of the mediation of Christ, that you may prevail.

**11. By the fire which burnt down the city — God calls upon London, by the voice of his judgments, to PREPARE FOR GREATER TROUBLES.** The *face of God* seems to threaten greater troubles; there is little sign that *God's brow* is smoothed now, more than it was before the fire; there is little evidence of the appeasement of God's anger; the face of the times seems to threaten greater troubles. The cloud over London and England is still very black — and seems to be thicker than it was before!

(1.) *God's own people* are likely to undergo greater troubles. Some of them have endured much — but they are likely to endure much more. Some of them have suffered deeply — but they are likely to suffer greater things more generally.

They have been brought low by affliction — but not as low as *others* are. When others of God's people are stripped of all — they enjoy a comparative prosperity.

They are not so low as they *deserve* to be; their Gospel-reproaching sins deserve far greater severities.

They are not so low as they may have *need* to be; they may need greater troubles, to unite them more one to another in their affections, to further their sanctification, to wean and loosen them more from the world; to humble them for, and purify them more from sin; to exercise and brighten more their graces.

They are not so low as possibly they *must* be, before they be exalted. The night is the darkest before the day breaks; the storm is the fiercest many times in its last blast; and the afflictions of God's people are the sorest — before God gives them deliverance. God lays his people most low — when he intends their highest exaltation! Surely, the expected shock is not yet over, and God's people's most dreadful sufferings seem most immediately to be threatened, they seem to be near, very near, even at the doors.

The intent of the late judgments by plague and fire, seems plainly to be for the fitting and preparing of them for more sharp and heavy strokes. If God had permitted those expected sufferings to have come upon them more *suddenly* — they might have found them more *unready*. God has given them time to prepare, and awakening warnings to prepare; and when will they be ready to suffer like Christians — if now they be not ready?

(2.) The *profane and wicked generation* in the land, are likely to endure greater troubles, as has been shown. And when the storm of God's anger breaks down upon them, are there no drops likely to fall upon London? Is not the whole land likely to be in danger of ruin, when God deals with the *ungodly and wicked crew*, whom he spares for some time, while he punishes so severely the more righteous?

The troubles of London have been great — but methinks it is evident, that London is in danger of greater troubles; therefore they have need to make preparation, which they have had such awakening calls unto.

Some possibly may think the bitterness of London's troubles is over, because their troubles have been so bitter; that the sharp winter cold is gone; but March can bring in as cold nipping frost as December and January did; and when the *spring of prosperity* is expected by some — they may find the sharpest part of the *winter of troubles* to be ahead of them. Prepare, therefore, London, for greater troubles!

**12. By the fire which burnt down the city — God expects that London should trust no more in *arms of flesh* — but in himself alone.** By these judgments, God has shown to London the weakness and insufficiency of *arms of flesh* — what broken reeds they are.

Some put their trust in **men**, and their great expectation of relief and comfort has been from their friends; by the plague God has shown, how frail and weak man is — how like grass, or a flower, that quickly withers, or is cut down — how like glass, or a bubble, which is easily broken and vanishes! Many have lost, by the plague, their chief friends upon whom they have had all their dependance; and the Lord has shown how insufficient a foundation *man* is, for any one's trust and confidence. Therefore he calls aloud to London, to "cease from man, whose breath is in his nostrils, for wherein is he to be accounted of?" Isaiah 2:22, not to trust in "any of the sons of men, in whom there is no help;" and the reason is, because "their breath goes forth, and they return to their dust; in that very day all their thoughts perish!" Psalm 146:3, 4.

Some put their trust in their **wealth** and **riches**, Proverbs 18:11. "The wealth of the rich is their fortified city; they imagine it an unscalable wall." God has by the fire, which has consumed so much of the wealth of the city, shown how insufficient a foundation *wealth* is, for any man's confidence. He has made it evident that riches are uncertain, and that they fly away with eagles' wings, sometimes while the owners are looking on! May not that which is threatened in Psalm 52:5, 7, be spoken of many in London, that God has routed some of them by the *plague*, out of the land of the living, plucked and forced others out of their habitations by the fire, and taken away their stay and prop from them; of whom it may be said, "Surely God will bring you down to everlasting ruin: He will snatch you up and tear you from your tent; he will uproot you from the land of the living. Here now is the man who did not make God his stronghold but trusted in his great wealth."

London, trust no more in arms of flesh — but trust in God alone: "It is better to trust in the Lord, than to put confidence in men; it is better to trust in the Lord, than to put confidence in princes," Psalm 117:8, 9. God is *knocking off your fingers* from all things here below; his will is that you should put your trust in him; which is one promised effect of great desolations and afflictions, which you should labor after; Zeph. 3:12. "I will also leave in the midst of you an afflicted and poor people — and they shall trust in the name of the Lord."

You were not so forward to trust in the Lord when you had greater abundance; endeavor to trust in him, now you are brought into greater poverty and affliction. His infinite power, wisdom, loving-kindness, his promise, truth, and faithfulness — are a strong foundation for your trust and confidence in God.

Trust in him at all *times*, in the worst of times; when your danger is greatest, he will be your "help and shield," Psalm 115:1. He will be your *refuge* under oppression, and "present help in time of trouble," Psalm 46:1. He will be your *rock* and *fortress*, your *high tower* to defend you, your deliverer to redeem you out of all your troubles.

Trust in God alone for all *things*: if you make use of creatures, do not lean and trust upon them, for they will slip from under you! But fix yourselves on God. O the peace and quiet which this will yield in shaking, troublesome days. When others' hearts tremble within them, and *shake like leaves* upon the approach of danger, "You shall not be afraid of evil tidings — but have your hearts fixed, trusting in the Lord," Psalm 112:7.

**18. By the fire which burnt down the city — God expects that London should have DEATH in continual remembrance.** This God expects from the judgments of the plague — the death of so many thousands a week in London, gave such a *spectacle of mortality*, and preached such a sermon in the city, as should bring the remembrance of death into their minds every day of their lives! The death, if it were but of one or two, should put you in mind of your latter end; but when you have seen so *many* go down into the pit before you — it should inscribe the remembrance of death more deeply upon your minds, the record of which you should look daily into.

The gates of the city, in the year of the *plague*, seemed to have this inscription upon them, *"All flesh is grass!"* Let that word sound every day in your ears, and remember your bodies are exposed to the stroke of death every day! And though you have out-lived the *plague*, that yet *death* has you in the chase, and will before long, (you know not how soon), overtake you! Remember that your hour-glass is running, and will quickly be run out; and therefore "all the days of your appointed time," as you should remember, so you should "prepare for your great change," Job 14:14.

God expects that the remaining inhabitants of London should be prepared well for death now, when they have had death so much in their view. Some of you have been sick of the plague, and brought to the very *brink* of the grave. All of you have been in danger of the plague, when the disease was so sore and raging. I fear most of you were unprepared for death at that time, and had you died then — that it would have been with horror. And I believe that there are few of you but did, in the time of your fears and danger, make *vows* and *promises*, if the Lord would shelter you from the *arrows* which flew about you, and spare your lives then — that you would lead new lives, and be more careful to prepare for your last change, so that death should not take you so unprovided anymore. God expects the *fulfilling* of your promises; and that you should *live up to the vows*, which you made in the time of your distress; and so provide for yourselves while you are well — that the *messenger of death* may have a welcome reception, whenever he summons you to leave this world.

**14. By the fire which burnt down the city — God expects that London should retain great impressions of ETERNITY.** You have had the *door of eternity* set wide open in your view, when so many were thronging in at the door; and I believe you had deeper apprehensions of eternity in those days, than ever you had in your lives! Take heed that those impressions do not wear off, and that you do not lose those apprehensions, especially when you are drawing every day nearer and nearer to eternity.

Think often of the *vast ocean of eternity*, without bottom or bank on the other side, into which the *whole stream of time* will empty itself; and how quickly the *small rivulet of your appointed days* may fall into it! Think often of the *unalterable state of joy or misery*, which you must enter into at the end of your course! Think how thin and short the pleasures of sin are in this life, in comparison of the horrible and endless torments of Hell! Think how "light and momentary the afflictions of God's people are here — in comparison with the exceeding and eternal weight of glory prepared for them in Heaven," 2 Corinthians 12:7.

**15. By the fire which burnt down the city — God calls upon London to secure themselves against the fire of HELL.**

London's fire was dreadful — but the fire of Hell will be a thousand-fold more dreadful!

The fire of London was kindled by man — but the fire of Hell will be kindled by God Himself! "Topheth has long been prepared; it has been made ready for the king. Its fire pit has been made deep and wide, with an abundance of fire and wood; the breath of the Lord, like a stream of burning sulfur, sets it ablaze!" Isaiah 30:33

The fire of London burnt the houses of the city, and consumed much of the goods; but the fire of Hell will burn the wicked themselves, "Depart, you cursed ones, into everlasting fire!" Matthew 25:41.

The fire of London burned most — but not all of the houses in the city; some are yet remaining — but the fire of Hell will burn all the wicked, not one of them shall escape and remain!

The fire of London was extinguished, and lasted but four days — but the fire of Hell will be inextinguishable, it will burn forever! It is called everlasting fire, in which the damned must lie and burn eternally, without any possibility of ever getting forth.

If you had known before of London's fire, where it would begin, and how it would spread, and seize upon your houses — surely you would have taken some course for the prevention of it. You surely know now of the fire of Hell — the Word of God has revealed it. O take some course for preventing of it, at least for securing of yourselves against it.

When the fire was burning in London you fled from it, lest it should have consumed your body as well as houses. O fly from the fire of Hell, into which you will be thrown, if you go on in sin! Flee from the wrath which is to come! Flee unto Jesus Christ, who alone can deliver you!

**16. By the fire which burnt down the city — God calls upon Londoners to be like STRANGERS and PILGRIMS in the world.**
God has burned you out of your habitations — that he might loosen your affections from houses, and riches, and all things here below; that he might unsettle you, unhinge, unfix you; that you might never think of rest and settlement in creatures, as long as you live. God calls upon you by this judgment, to take off your hearts from this *world*, which is so very uncertain — and to be

like strangers and pilgrims upon the earth, who are to take up your lodging here but a few days and nights in your passage to the other world.

God expects you should live as those who have here no certain dwelling-place; and therefore that you should not lavish away too much of your thoughts, and affections, and time, about these *uncertain things*, which are of so short a continuance, and with which you cannot have a long abode.

God has by his judgments, crucified the world very much before you, and he expects that the world should be crucified in you. God has poured contempt upon the world, and set a mark of disgrace thereon. He has cast dirt upon the face, where you imagined before so much beauty to lie; and he expects that you should fall in esteem, and grow out of love with the world, and never go a-whoring from him to the creatures anymore!

**17. By the fire which burnt down the city — God calls upon London to make HIM their habitation.** Psalm 90:1, "Lord, *you* have been our dwelling-place in all generations." God is the *hiding-place*, and he is the *dwelling-place* of his people. You have lost your dwelling by the fire — make God your habitation, and dwell in him, to whom you may have constant resort, and in whom you may have a sure abode. Get possession of this house, by your union to God through his Son; and when you are in, keep possession, abide in this house, do not wander from him, and turn yourselves out of doors, by breaking of his household laws. Make God your *home*, and labor to be much acquainted at home. Spend your time with God, and give your hearts to him. Rest and repose yourselves in God daily — look for all your provisions in him, and from him. Walk in him, and with him. Make God your habitation.

**18. By the fire which burnt down the city — God calls upon London to seek after an ABIDING CITY.** Hebrews 13:14, "We have no continuing city — but we seek one to come." London has reason to say the former, therefore let London do the latter. You have seen the city fall by the fire — seek after a city which has more lasting foundations, and is of such strong building, that time cannot wear and weaken it, nor can flames of fire reach and consume it! I mean the New Jerusalem, which is above, the Heavenly city, whose builder and maker is God — there are mansions, *abiding places* for the saints, John 14:2. There the wicked will cease from troubling, and the weary will be at rest! Seek after this city, labor for a title to it, lay up your treasure in it, get your affections set upon it! Above all trades — drive a trade with Heaven, which, in the outcome, will yield you the best returns!

**19. By the fire which burnt down the city — God expects that London should labor to BUILD HIS HOUSE.** The neglect of God's house, I believe, has been a great cause of the fall of so many houses in the city by fire. God expects that now you should endeavor the building of his house; otherwise, I do not think that God will again build your houses. You may have an Act of Parliament for building the city, and set workmen about it; but unless God enacts it, the building will never go forward; unless God builds the city — the workmen will labor in vain! Read and consider the *prophecy of Haggai.* Set about the work of reformation more vigorously; especially in the house and worship of God.

**20. By the fire which burnt down the city — God expects that Londoners should DEDICATE themselves and families unto him.** You have broken your baptismal and other vows, and God has made great breaches upon you for your infidelity; now renew your vows, give up yourselves to God, avouch him to be your God, and avouch yourselves to be his people, and live accordingly. Take up Joshua's resolution, that whatever others in the land do, *that you and your families will serve the Lord.* Make it your only business in the world, to serve God. Let true religion have an influence upon all your actions. Do nothing without the warrant of God's precept. Let your lives be such as befit the Gospel; govern your families in the fear of God. Learn more righteousness by God's judgments, and be quickened by them unto a more holy and strict walking.

And if you yield such *fruits* as these, which God expects after his *plowing* and *harrowing* of you; if you open your ear to the "Terrible voice of the Lord," which has uttered itself "in the city," and with full purpose of heart set about the practice of the duties he expects and calls for — then you may hope that he will yet build you up, and plant you, that he will close your breaches, and raise up your ruinous habitations; that he will make you glad according to the years wherein he has afflicted you, and allow you to see good days, instead of those evil days which you have seen and felt. Then the Lord will rejoice over you to do you good; and make London like Mount Zion, where he will pitch his tent, and take up his habitation! Then he will compass you about with the bulwark of salvation, and prevent those further utterly desolating judgments which you are in danger of. Yes, the Lord will be a *wall of fire* round about you, and the glory in the midst of London, from whence his praise and your fame shall sound throughout the whole world!

Lightning Source UK Ltd.
Milton Keynes UK
UKHW022202270420
362388UK00014B/3244

9 781612 036298